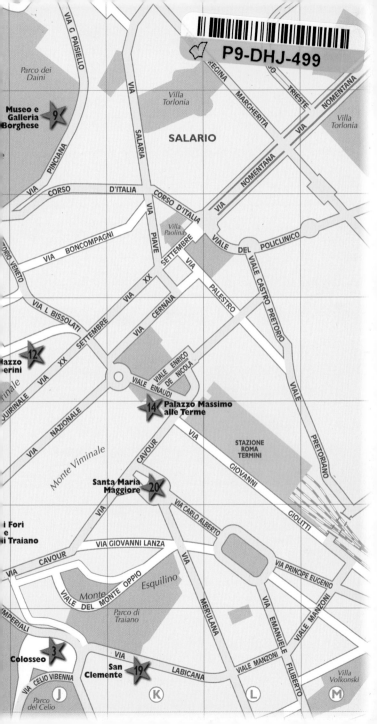

Fodor's
25 Best

ROME

Contents

KEY TO SYMBOLS

➕ Map reference to the accompanying pull-out map

✉ Address

☎ Telephone number

🕐 Opening/closing times

🍴 Restaurant or café

🚉 Nearest rail station

Ⓜ Nearest Metro (subway) station

🚌 Nearest bus route

ENTERTAINMENT 128

Whether you're after a cultural fix or just want a place to relax with a drink after a hard day's sight-seeing, we've made the best choices for you.

EAT 138

Uncover great dining experiences, from a quick bite at lunch to top-notch evening meals.

SLEEP 152

We've brought together the best hotels in the city, whatever budget you're on.

NEED TO KNOW 160

The practical information you need to make your trip run smoothly.

PULL-OUT MAP

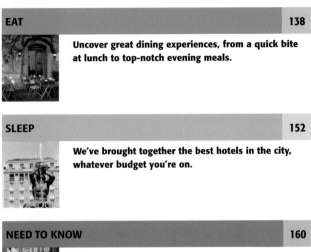

The pull-out map accompanying this book is a comprehensive street plan of the city. We've given grid references within the book for each sight and listing.

📷 Nearest riverboat or ferry stop

♿ Facilities for visitors with disabilities

ℹ️ Tourist information

❷ Other practical information

🔲 Admission charges: Expensive (over €8), Moderate (€4–€8) and Inexpensive (under €4)

▷ Further information

Introducing Rome

Rome is one of the world's great cities, the city of the Caesars, of romance and *la dolce vita*, of long, hot, sunny days, of superb art galleries, churches and museums, of fountain-splashed piazzas and majestic monuments to its golden age of empire.

It is also a city with all the myriad pleasures of any Italian destination—notably superb food and wine—as well as great bars, cafés, and shopping, vibrant nightlife and numerous cultural events. At the same time, Rome is very much a contemporary city—traffic rumbles around medieval cobbled streets—though the skyline bristles not with glittering skyscrapers but with the domes of churches and palaces.

But how to visit a city where there is so much to see? First of all don't rush to the Colosseum, St. Peter's or the Sistine Chapel on your first morning. Rome for much of the year is hot and crowded. If you try to cram in too much, or soldier on through the heat, the chances are you'll emerge battered rather than enraptured. Instead, stroll around the Ghetto or Trastevere, two of the city's quaintest old quarters, or have a cappuccino in one of Rome's loveliest squares, Campo de' Fiori or Piazza Navona. Or head for one of the lesser-known art-filled churches, such as San Luigi dei Francesi or Santa Maria del Popolo, crammed with masterpieces by Raphael, Pinturicchio and Caravaggio.

Once gently acclimatized, and hopefully charmed by the city's quieter side, then you can begin to think about the Trevi Fountain, the Spanish Steps, the Roman Forum or the Vatican Museums. And, of course, the newer but still relatively unsung museums that have opened in the last few years—notably the Palazzo Altemps and Palazzo Massimo alle Terme, both devoted to Classical art and sculpture, or the MAXXI gallery, an architectural *tour de force* given over to contemporary art. But bear in mind this is a living city with more than 3,000 years of history. One, two, even ten visits aren't enough to do it justice. However much you see, one thing is for certain, you'll be back.

FACTS AND FIGURES

- Population estimate in 2013: 2,617,175.
- The official age of Rome in 2014 is 2,768 years.
- There have been 266 popes and 73 emperors.
- The city covers an area of 1,494sq km (577sq miles).
- Vatican City covers an area of 0.44sq km (0.17sq miles) and is the world's smallest state.

SECRET KEYHOLE

Rome's most charming view is from Piazza dei Cavalieri di Malta on the Aventine Hill. To find it, go to the left of the church of Santa Sabina and to the end of the piazza; look through the keyhole of the door (No. 3) of the Priory of the Knights of Malta. Through this tiny hole you will see a secret garden and an avenue of trees framing...but let's not spoil the surprise: see for yourself.

WATERY WASTE

More than 50 of Rome's fountains are fed by the waters of the Aqua Virgo, a source that the Romans first brought into the city in 19BC. It flows from the countryside outside the city, and feeds the Barcaccia fountain at the foot of the Spanish Steps, before supplying many others, including the most famous of them all, the Fontana di Trevi.

SWISS GUARD

The pope's official bodyguards are recruited from Switzerland's four predominantly Catholic cantons. Each must be between 19 and 25, at least 1.75m (5ft 9in) tall and remain unmarried during their tour of duty. Their distinctive uniforms were designed by Michelangelo in the hues of the Medici popes—red, yellow and blue.

Focus On Bernini

Many have changed the face of Rome over the centuries—artists, emperors, tyrants and popes—but few have had a more lasting or more widespread effect on the very fabric of the city than Gian Lorenzo Bernini, a sculptor and architect whose piazzas, sculptures, follies and fountains you will encounter time and again in the Eternal City.

Papal Favour

Bernini was born in Naples in 1598, the son of Angelica Galante and Pietro Bernini, a Florentine sculptor. At the age of seven he was accompanying his father to Rome and assisting him in artistic commissions, work that eventually brought him to the attention of Pope Paul V and the Pope's affluent nephew, Cardinal Scipione Borghese. The patronage of the papacy and of wealthy Roman families such as the Borghese was the key for any artist hoping to work and succeed in Rome, especially in the era of the baroque, when the city's churches, palaces and public spaces were undergoing a dramatic transformation.

Bernini's output would be prodigious, and he would go on to work under several popes, combining undoubted talent with a shrewd awareness of how to play his wealthy patrons. In this he was in distinct contrast to his rival of the period, Francesco Borromini, a more inventive architect, but a troubled soul whose dark disposition won him few friends and fewer commissions.

St. Peter's

Bernini's mark on Rome is most apparent in its principal religious building, St. Peter's (▷ 14–15), where he designed the great piazza in front of the church, parts of the facade and much of the interior, including the colossal *baldacchino,* or canopy, above the altar. He also designed the church of Sant'Andrea al

Clockwise from top left: The Rape of Proserpina, *Museo e Galleria Borghese; Fontana del Nettuno, Piazza Navona;* Apollo and Daphne, *Museo e Galleria*

Quirinale and had a hand in several palaces, notably the Palazzo Barberini (▷ 36–37), Palazzo Montecitorio and Palazzo Chigi-Odaleschi. And when you stop to admire a fountain in Rome, the chances are that it will be the work of Bernini, from the most prominent—the Fontana dei Quattro Fiumi in Piazza Navona (▷ 46–47)—to more idiosyncratic fancies such as the Barcaccia fountain (▷ 48–49) at the foot of the Spanish Steps, and the Fontana delle Api and Fontana del Tritone (▷ 67) in Piazza Barberini.

Masterpieces

Bernini's consummate architectural skill was in creating public spaces, as in the Piazza San Pietro, or adapting existing churches and palaces in ways that were sympathetic to their surroundings. His sculptural skills—and he was the foremost sculptor of his day and the greatest since Michelangelo—were a peerless technique and the ability to capture a narrative moment in stone.

Both dramatic and dynamic qualities can be seen best in his masterpieces in the Galleria Borghese (▷ 30–31), housed in the sumptuous palace of his old patron, Cardinal Scipione Borghese. Here is David caught in the act of casting his sling at Goliath; Daphne turning into a laurel tree to escape the clutches of Apollo; the abductor's hand sinking into the soft thigh of his victim in *The Rape of Proserpina*. These are dazzling, virtuoso works, intended to impress, but Bernini can also be witty and quiet, and it is his smaller works you'll find dotted around Rome that you may well remember best after you leave the city: the charming tortoises added to the Fontana delle Tartarughe (▷ 67), for example, or his 'Breezy Angels' on the Ponte Sant'Angelo and the quaint little elephant and obelisk in front of Santa Maria sopra Minerva (▷ 54–55).

Borghese; angel on Ponte Sant'Angelo; detail of the baldacchino, St. Peter's Basilica; David, Museo e Galleria Borghese; the colonnade, St. Peter's Square

Top Tips For...

These great suggestions will help you to tailor your ideal visit to Rome, no matter how you choose to spend your time.

...Burning the Midnight Oil
Sit up late with the beautiful people in **Caffè della Pace** (▷ 144).
Share a glass of wine with the characters in the bars around **Campo de' Fiori** (▷ 44–45).
Visit one or more of the many clubs in the **Testaccio** (▷ 130, 132) nightlife district.

...Saving for a Rainy Day
Buy an integrated **travel pass** (▷ 167) and save on public transport.
Visit Rome's art-crammed churches, such as **Santa Maria sopra Minerva** (▷ 54–55), they are virtually all free.
Time your visit for the last Sunday of the month, when the normally expensive **Vatican Museums** (▷ 26–27) are free.

...An Evening of Entertainment
See what's playing at the **Teatro dell'Opera di Roma** (▷ 137), Rome's opera house.
Enjoy a night of blues or jazz at the long-established **Big Mama** (▷ 134).
Look out for posters advertising **church recitals** and other **classical music concerts**. In summer, many are held outdoors (▷ 131).

...Romantic Suppers
Dine outdoors in summer; try **Panattoni** (▷ 149), but almost any restaurant or pizzeria with tables on a terrace will do.
Splash out on a meal at **Il Convivio Troiani** (▷ 145), for that special dining experience.
Buy a picnic and take it to the **Pincio gardens** (▷ 71) to watch the sunset over St. Peter's.

...Speciality Shopping
Via dei Coronari (▷ panel 120) and nearby streets for antiques and sumptuous fabrics.

Clockwise from top left: Cafés in Piazza Navona buzz at night; ruined palaces on the Palatine Hill; dining at Giggetto in the Ghetto district; enjoy a coffee at

Stroll down **Via Margutta** to take in its various art galleries (▷panel, 120).
For designer clothes and accessories, it has to be **Via dei Condotti** (▷ 120–121).

…A Breath of Fresh Air
The **Villa Borghese** (▷ 75) park offers numerous walks and shady nooks.
Escape the crowds around the Forum by climbing the **Palatine Hill** (▷ 69).
If you don't have time to see the Gianicolo and Villa Doria Pamphilj above Trastevere, how about the closer **Orto Botanico** (▷ 70)?

…A Taste of Tradition
Giggetto (▷ 147) and **Piperno** (▷ 149) serve classic Roman-Jewish cuisine.
As its name suggests, **Checchino dal 1887** (▷ 145) has been serving traditional Roman food for more than 120 years.
To sample pizza at its best, try **Ivo** (▷ 148) and **Da Baffetto** (▷ 145), which have served pizza to generations of Romans.

…A Great Cup of Coffee
La Tazza d'Oro (▷ 151), a stone's throw from the Pantheon, is a temple to the espresso.
Sant'Eustachio (▷ 150) serves what many consider to be Rome's best cup of coffee.
Antico Caffè del Brasile (▷ 142) knows its beans—Pope John Paul II once bought his coffee here.

…The World's Best Classical Sculpture
Visit the **Palazzo Altemps** (▷ 34–35) and **Palazzo Massimo alle Terme** (▷ 40–41), which have beautifully presented collections.
To see individual sculptural works go to the **Musei Capitolini** (▷ 24–25), with some of the city's most significant pieces.
The **Laocoön** (▷ 27) is the most celebrated of the Vatican Museums' immense collection of sculptures.

Sant'Eustachio; the head of Constantine in the Musei Capitolini; window-shop in style in Via dei Condotti; Bernini's elephant statue with the Pantheon behind

Timeline

753BC Traditional date of the foundation of Rome by Romulus, first of the city's seven kings.

616–578BC Tarquinius Priscus, Rome's first Etruscan king.

509BC Etruscans expelled and the Roman Republic founded.

60BC Rome ruled by a triumvirate of Pompey, Marcus Licinius Crassus and Julius Caesar.

PUNIC WARS

The First Punic War against Carthage (North Africa) started in 264BC and lasted for around 23 years. In the Second Punic War (218–201BC) Rome was threatened by Hannibal, leader of the Carthaginian army. But Rome finally defeated Carthage in the Third Punic War (149–146BC).

RELIGION

There are 280 churches within the city walls and 94 per cent of Romans have had their children baptized. However, only 23 per cent of Romans attend Mass.

48BC Caesar declared ruler for life but assassinated by rivals in 44BC.

27BC–AD14 Rule of Octavian, Caesar's great nephew, who as Augustus becomes the first Roman emperor.

98–117 Reign of Emperor Trajan. Military campaigns extend the Empire's boundaries.

284–286 Empire divided into East and West.

306–337 The Emperor Constantine reunites the Empire, legalizing Christianity. St. Peter's and the first Christian churches are built.

410 Rome is sacked by the Goths led by Alaric I.

476 Romulus Augustulus is the last Western Roman Emperor.

800 Charlemagne awards some territories to papacy; Pope Leo III crowns him Holy Roman Emperor.

The Arch of Constantine, on the route of the marathon in the 1960 Olympic Games

Caius Julius Caesar

CAIUS JULIUS CÆSAR.

1508 Michelangelo begins the Sistine Chapel ceiling.

1527 Rome is sacked by German and Spanish troops under the Holy Roman Emperor, Charles V.

1848 Uprisings in Rome under Mazzini and Garibaldi force Pope Pius IX to flee. The new Roman Republic is defeated by the French in 1849 and the papacy restored.

1870 Rome joins a united Italy.

1929 Lateran Treaty recognizes the Vatican as a separate state.

1940 Italy enters World War II.

1960 Rome hosts the Olympic Games.

2000 Some 30 million pilgrims visit Rome for the millennial jubilee year.

2005 Pope John Paul II dies, after 26 years as pontiff, and is succeeded by Pope Benedict XVI.

2006 Silvio Berlusconi, Italy's longest serving post-war Prime Minister, is replaced by Romano Prodi of the centre left party.

2011 Mario Monti, who leads a technocratic government designed to address Italy's economic problems, becomes Prime Minister.

2013 Jorge Maria Bergoglio, born in Buenos Aires, is elected pope and takes the name Francis I.

WHAT'S IN A NAME

Many of Rome's street names include dates that allude to significant events in the city's history. Via XX Settembre (20 September) remembers that day in 1870 when Italian troops liberated Rome: The city became the country's capital in the same year. Via XXIV Maggio (24 May) recalls the day in 1915 that Italy entered World War I. Via IV Novembre (4 November) alludes to the date of the Italian armistice and victory in 1918 after World War I. And Via XXV Aprile (25 April) commemorates the day in 1944 that the Allies liberated the city from Nazi rule.

Detail of the ceiling of the Sistine Chapel painted by Michelangelo

Pope Francis I was elected in 2013

Top 25

This section contains the must-see Top 25 sights and experiences in Rome. They are listed alphabetically, and numbered so you can locate them on the inside front cover map.

TOP 25

HIGHLIGHTS

- St. Peter's Square, surrounded by 284 columns
- Swiss Guards
- Dome
- *Pietà,* Michelangelo
- The 25.5m (83ft) 13th-century BC Egyptian obelisk, brought here in the first century AD
- *St. Peter,* Arnolfo di Cambio
- Monument to Pope Alexander VII, Bernini

TIP

- You have to join what can be very long lines for security checks (on the right or left side of Piazza San Pietro) before entering the basilica.

Although some of the works of art in St. Peter's can be rather disappointing, the interior impresses as the spiritual capital of Roman Catholicism with an overwhelming sense of scale and decorative glory.

The creators The first St. Peter's was built by Constantine around AD326, reputedly on the site where St. Peter was buried following his crucifixion in AD64. By 1452 the church was in such a state of disrepair that Pope Nicholas V resolved to build a new basilica. After several false starts it was virtually rebuilt to plans by Bramante, and then again to designs by Antonio da Sangallo, Giacomo della Porta, Michelangelo and Carlo Maderno. Michelangelo was also responsible for much of the dome, and Bernini finished the facade and the interior.

Left: The far-reaching views from the dome take in St. Peter's Square with its central obelisk, Bernini's impressive symmetrical colonnades and Rome beyond; below: The famous dome of St Peter's Basilica, designed by Michelangelo, is floodlit at night

What to see Michelangelo's unforgettable *Pietà* (1499)—which is behind glass following an attack in 1972—is in the first chapel of the right nave. At the end of the same nave stands a statue of St. Peter: His right foot has been caressed by millions since 1857 when Pius IX granted a 50-day indulgence to anyone kissing it following confession. Bernini's colossal sculpted bronze *baldacchino*, or high altar canopy, (1624–33), was built during the papacy of Urban VIII, a scion of the Barberini family; it is decorated with bees, the Barberini's dynastic symbol. To its rear are Guglielmo della Porta's Tomb of Paul III (left) and Bernini's influential Tomb of Urban VIII (right). Rome seen from the dome (the entrance is at the end of the right nave, past the Holy Door) is the highlight of a visit.

THE BASICS

www.vatican.va

✚ C4

✉ Piazza San Pietro, Città del Vaticano

☎ 06 6988 1662/3731

🕐 Apr–Sep daily 7–7; Oct–Mar 7–6. Dome Apr–Sep daily 8–6; Oct–Mar 8–5. Grottos Mon–Sat 9–3.30

🍽 Shop

Ⓜ Ottaviano

🚌 64 to Porta Cavalleggeri or 23, 32, 49, 492, 990 to Piazza del Risorgimento

♿ Wheelchair access

💶 Basilica free. Dome moderate. Grottos expensive

Castel Sant'Angelo, rising above the river, has served as imperial tomb, a papal citadel, medieval prison and army barracks. Today the 58-room museum traces the castle's nearly 2,000-year history, providing a contrast to the Vatican Museums.

Many incarnations The Castel Sant'Angelo was built by Emperor Hadrian in AD130 as a mausoleum for himself, his family and his dynastic successors. It was crowned by a gilded chariot driven by a statue of Hadrian disguised as the sun god Apollo. Emperors were buried in its vaults until about AD271, when under threat of invasion from Germanic raiders it became a citadel and was incorporated into the city's walls. Its present name arose in AD590, after a vision by Gregory the Great, who while leading

Clockwise from far left: The 18th-century statue atop the fortress is by Flemish sculptor Pieter Verschaffelt; the building has been a mausoleum, fortress, papal prison and museum; Ponte Sant'Angelo, the route to the castle, watched over by Bernini's angels; view of the Tiber from the terrace

a procession through Rome to pray for the end of plague saw an angel sheathing a sword on this spot, an act thought to symbolize the end of the pestilence.

Castle and museum In AD847 Leo IV converted the building into a papal fortress, and in 1277 Nicholas III linked it to the Vatican by a passageway, the *passetto*. Used as a prison in the Renaissance, and then an army barracks after 1870, the castle became a museum in 1933. Exhibits, spread over four floors, are scattered around a confusing, but fascinating, array of rooms and corridors. Best of these is the beautiful Sala Paolina, done with stucco, fresco and *trompe-l'oeil*. The most memorable sight is the 360-degree view from the castle's terrace, the setting for the last act of Puccini's *Tosca*.

THE BASICS

www.castelsantangelo.
beniculturali.it

⊞ E4

✉ Lungotevere Castello 50

☎ 06 681 9111; ticket office 06 689 6003 online at www.gebart.it

🕐 Tue–Sun 9–7.30

🍴 Café

Ⓜ Lepanto

🚌 30, 49, 70, 87, 130, 186, 224, 492, 926, 990 to Piazza Cavour or the Lungotevere

♿ Poor

💶 Moderate

3 Colosseo

HIGHLIGHTS

● Circumference walls
● Arches: 80 lower arches for the easy admission of crowds
● Doric columns: lowest arcade
● Ionic columns: central arcade
● Corinthian columns: upper arcade
● Underground cells
● Sockets that once housed binding metal clamps
● *Vomitoria*: interior exits and entrances
● Views of ancient Rome from the upper levels

TIP

● The Colosseum's ticket office can be very busy—buy your ticket at the Palatine or Foro Romano to avoid waiting, or online.

The Pantheon may be better preserved and the Forum more historically important, but no monument in Rome rivals the majesty of the Colosseum, the largest surviving structure from Roman antiquity.

Awe-inspiring The Colosseum was begun by Emperor Vespasian in AD72 and inaugurated by his son, Titus, in AD80 with a gala that saw 5,000 animals slaughtered in a day (and 100 days of continuous games thereafter). Finishing touches to the 55,000-seat stadium were added by Domitian (AD81–96). Three types of columns support the arcades, and the walls are made of brick and volcanic tufa faced with marble blocks. Its long decline began in the Middle Ages, with the pillaging of stone to build churches and palaces. The desecration ended

Clockwise from far left: The Colosseum takes its name from the Colossus of Nero, a bronze statue that once stood close by; the four storeys above ground contained seating for spectators, while underground was a maze of corridors, cells and animal pens; mosaic of gladiatorial fighting

in 1744, when the structure was consecrated in memory of the Christians supposedly martyred in the arena (later research suggests they weren't). Clearing of the site and excavations began late in the 19th century.

Games Armed combat at the Colosseum went on for some 500 years. Criminals, slaves and gladiators fought each other or wild animals, often to the death, and mock sea battles were waged (the arena could be flooded via underground pipes). Spectators exercised the power of life and death over defeated combatants, by waving handkerchiefs to show mercy or displaying a down-turned thumb to demand the finishing stroke. Survivors' throats were often cut anyway, and the dead were poked with a red-hot iron to make sure they had expired.

THE BASICS

➕ J7
✉ Piazza del Colosseo, Via dei Fori Imperiali
☎ 06 3996 7700; online at www.coopculture.it
🕐 mid-Feb–mid-Mar 8.30–5; mid-end Mar closes 7.30; Apr–Aug 8.30–7.15, Sep 8.30–7; Oct–mid-Feb 8.30–6.30
🚇 Colosseo
🚌 3, 60, 75, 85, 87, 117 to Piazza del Colosseo
♿ Poor to the interior; limited access from Via Celio Vibenna entrance
💶 Expensive (joint ticket with Monte Palatino and Foro Romano)

HIGHLIGHTS

- *Oceanus*
- *Allegory of Health* (right of *Oceanus*)
- *Virgin Indicating the Spring to Soldiers*
- *Allegory of Abundance* (left of *Oceanus*)
- *Agrippa Approving the Design of the Aqueduct*
- *Triton with Horse* (on the right, symbolizing the ocean in repose)
- *Triton with Horse* (on the left, symbolizing a tempestuous sea)
- Facade of Santi Vincenzo e Anastasio
- Baroque interior of Santa Maria in Trivio

There is no lovelier surprise than that which confronts you as you emerge from the tight warren of streets around the Trevi Fountain, the city's most famous fountain—a sight 'silvery to the eye and ear', in the words of Charles Dickens.

Virgin discovery In its earliest guise the Trevi Fountain lay at the end of the Aqua Virgo, or Acqua Vergine, an aqueduct built by Agrippa in 19BC (supposedly filled with Rome's sweetest waters). The spring that fed it was reputedly discovered by a virgin, hence its name. (She is said to have shown her discovery to some Roman soldiers, a scene—along with Agrippa's approval of the aqueduct's plans—described in bas-reliefs on the fountain's second tier.) The fountain's liveliness and charm are embodied in

Clockwise from far left: The central figure of the fountain is Oceanus, god of the sea, in a chariot pulled by two winged horses; the impressive monument is a must for any visitor to Rome; this triton and winged horse symbolize calm waters; the fountain is particularly effective when floodlit at night

the pose of *Oceanus*, the central figure, and the two giant tritons and their horses (symbolizing a calm and a stormy sea) drawing his chariot. Other statues represent Abundance and Health and, above, the Four Seasons, which each carry gifts.

The fountains A new fountain was built in 1453, ordered by Pope Nicholas V, who paid for it by taxing wine. Its name came from the three roads *(tre vie)* that converged on the piazza. The present fountain was commissioned by Pope Clement XII in 1732 and finished in 1762: Its design was inspired by the Arch of Constantine and is attributed to Nicola Salvi, with possible contributions from Bernini. Those wishing to return to Rome toss a coin (over the shoulder) into the fountain.

THE BASICS

- ✚ G5
- ✉ Piazza Fontana di Trevi
- 🕐 Always open
- 🚇 Spagna or Barberini
- 🚌 C3, 52, 53, 61, 62, 71, 95, 117, 119 and other routes to Via del Corso and Via del Tritone
- ♿ Access via cobbled street
- ✋ Free

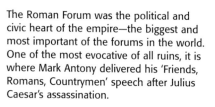

HIGHLIGHTS

● Temple of Antoninus and Faustina (AD141)
● Colonna di Foca (AD608)
● Arch of Septimius Severus (AD203)
● Curia (Senate House, 80BC)
● Portico of the Dei Consentes (AD367)
● Temple of Saturn (AD284)
● Santa Maria Antiqua, the Forum's oldest church, dating back to the fifth century AD
● Arch of Titus

TIPS

● Making sense of the Forum is quite a challenge—use an audioguide to get more out of your visit.
● Take something to drink as there are no bars in the Forum area.

The Roman Forum was the political and civic heart of the empire—the biggest and most important of the forums in the world. One of the most evocative of all ruins, it is where Mark Antony delivered his 'Friends, Romans, Countrymen' speech after Julius Caesar's assassination.

History The Forum (Foro Romano) started life as a marsh between the Palatine and Capitoline hills, taking its name from a word meaning 'outside the walls'. Later, it became a rubbish dump, and then, when drained, a marketplace and a religious shrine. In time it acquired all the structures of Rome's burgeoning civic, social and political life. Over the many centuries, consuls, emperors and senators have embellished it with magnificent temples, courts and basilicas.

Clockwise from far left: Ionic columns mark the front of the Temple of Saturn; the triumphal Arch of Titus was built in the first century AD to commemorate the Emperor's sack of Jerusalem; climb the Palatine Hill for views over the Roman Forum; relief detail on the Arch of Septimius Severus

Forum Two millennia of plunder and decay have left a mishmash of odd pillars and jumbled stones, which nonetheless can begin to make vivid sense given a plan and some imagination. The Rostrum, the setting for Mark Antony's famous speech, provided the platform for many great historic moments.

Beauty spots Today, orange trees, oleanders and cypresses line the paths, and grasses and wildflowers flourish among the ancient remains. Somewhat aloof from the rubble stands the elegantly restored House of the Vestal Virgins (Casa delle Vestali), home of a sect formed of daughters of the Roman nobility chosen to serve Vesta, goddess of hearth and home. There were always six in number, who served 30 years from age six to 36.

THE BASICS

✚ H7

✉ Entrance at Largo Romolo e Remo on Via dei Fori Imperiali

☎ 06 3996 7700 (Mon–Fri 9–6, Sat 9–2) or 06 0608; www.coopculture.it

🎫 As for Colosseum (▷ 19)

🚇 Colosseo

🚌 60, 75, 84, 85, 87, 117, 271, 571, 810, 850 to Via dei Fori Imperiali

♿ Access difficult to much of site

💶 Expensive. Joint ticket (valid 2 days) with Colosseo and Palatino

HIGHLIGHTS

Palazzo Nuovo
● Replica equestrian piazza statue of Marcus Aurelius
● *Capitoline Venus*: life-size statue of the goddess
● The colossal statue of river god Marforio above the fountain in the courtyard

Palazzo dei Conservatori
● Caravaggio's painting of St. John the Baptist
● Bronze of *Lupa Capitolina*
● The original, restored statue of Marcus Aurelius
● Giant head and fragments of Constantine's statue

TIP

● The top-floor café, accessible without paying the museum entrance fee, offers wonderful views of the city.

The outstanding Greek and Roman sculptures in the Capitoline Museums (Palazzo Nuovo and Palazzo dei Conservatori) make a far more accessible introduction to the subject than the Vatican Museums.

Palazzo Nuovo The Capitoline Museums occupy two palaces on opposite sides of the Piazza del Campidoglio and are linked by an underground passage. Both were restored earlier this century. Designed by Michelangelo, the Palazzo Nuovo (on the north side) contains most of the finest pieces. Few are more impressive than the magnificent equestrian statue of the emperor and philosopher Marcus Aurelius, which is, surprisingly, a well-made replica of the second-century AD original moved into the museum next door for restoration after damage

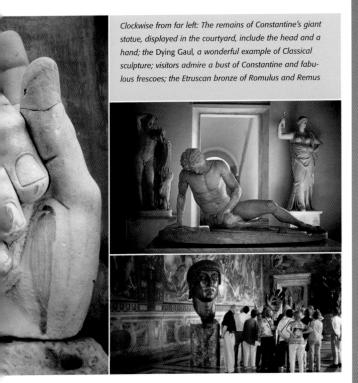

Clockwise from far left: The remains of Constantine's giant statue, displayed in the courtyard, include the head and a hand; the Dying Gaul, a wonderful example of Classical sculpture; visitors admire a bust of Constantine and fabulous frescoes; the Etruscan bronze of Romulus and Remus

in 1981. Among the sculptures inside are celebrated Roman copies in marble of Greek originals, including the *Dying Gaul*, *Wounded Amazon*, *Capitoline Venus* and the discus thrower *Discobolus*. In the Sala degli Imperatori is a portrait gallery of busts of Roman emperors.

Palazzo dei Conservatori As well as the Pinacoteca Capitolina art gallery and original Marcus Aurelius statue, the Conservatori is distinguished by a courtyard featuring the head and fragments of the fourth-century AD statue of Constantine, originally 12m (40ft) high. Also inside is the fifth-century BC Etruscan *Lupa Capitolina*, the she-wolf suckling Romulus and Remus (the twins were added by Antonio Pollaiuolo in 1510). Paintings include works by Caravaggio, Velázquez, Titian and Veronese.

THE BASICS

www.museicapitolini.org

⊕ G6

✉ Piazza del Campidoglio 1 (ticket office in Palazzo dei Conservatori)

☎ 06 0608; online booking www.ticketclic.it

🕐 Tue–Sun 9–8 (last admission 1 hour before closing)

🚍 40, 44, 64 and all other services to Piazza Venezia

♿ Poor: ramped steps to Piazza del Campidoglio

💰 Expensive; combined Capitolini Card available

25

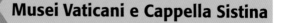

HIGHLIGHTS

- Michelangelo's fearsome depiction of God in the *Creation of Adam* in the Sistine Chapel
- Apollo del Belvedere (Museo Pio-Clementino)
- *Marte di Todi* (Museo Gregoriano-Etrusco)
- Maps Gallery (Galleria delle Carte Geografiche)
- Paintings in the Pinacoteca (Art Gallery)
- Room of the Animals (Museo Pio-Clementino)

TIPS

- Avoid waiting in long queues to get in by booking your tickets online.
- Don't become trapped in the waiting lines to see the Sistine Chapel—decide beforehand on your own priorities.

This is the largest and most impressive museum complex in the world, incorporating one of Michelangelo's supreme masterpieces in the Sistine Chapel.

Treasures of 12 museums At least two days (and 7km/4 miles of walking) are needed to do justice to the Vatican Museums. Egyptian and Assyrian art; Etruscan artefacts; the more esoteric anthropological collections; or modern religious art—whatever your priorities, several sights should not be missed. Most obvious are the four rooms of the Stanze di Raffaello, each of which is decorated with frescoes by Raphael. Further fresco cycles by Pinturicchio and Fra Angelico adorn the Borgia Apartment and Chapel of Nicholas V, and are complemented by an almost unmatched collection of paintings

Clockwise from far left: Giuseppe Momo's spiral staircase; the Laocoön group in the Museo Pio-Clementino; Michelangelo's ceiling in the Sistine Chapel; the Galleria della Carte Geografiche and, to the left, its decorated ceiling; detail of a fresco by Melozzo da Forlì in the Pinacoteca

in the Vatican Art Gallery. The best of the Greek and Roman sculpture is the breathtaking Laocoön group in the Cortile Ottagono of the Museo Pio-Clementino. The list of artists whose work is shown in the Collezione di Arte Religiosa Moderna is a roll call of the most famous in the last 100 years, from Pablo Picasso to Salvador Dalí and Henry Moore.

Sistine Chapel The chapel was built for Pope Sixtus IV between 1475 and 1483, but Pope Julius II commissioned Michelangelo to paint the ceiling of the Sistine Chapel in 1508. The frescoes, comprising more than 300 individual figures, were completed in four years. The extraordinary fresco behind the high altar, the *Last Judgement*, was begun for Pope Paul III in 1534 and completed in 1541.

THE BASICS

www.museivaticani.va

✚ C4

✉ Viale Vaticano 100, Città del Vaticano

☎ 06 6988 3322

🕐 Mon–Sat 9–6 (ticket office closes at 4); last Sun of month 9–2 (ticket offices closes 12.30)

🍴 Café, restaurant and shop

🚇 Cipro–Musei Vaticani

🚌 23, 32, 49, 81, 492, 990 to Piazza del Risorgimento, 40 to Piazza Pia or 64 to Porta Cavalleggeri

♿ Wheelchair access

💷 Very expensive (includes entry to all Vatican museums); free last Sun of month

27

8 Museo dei Fori Imperiali e Mercati di Traiano

HIGHLIGHTS

● The view of the 13th-century Torre delle Milizie
● The intricate spiral bas-relief that climbs Trajan's Column, depicting victories in battle
● The Basilica Ulpia, which became the most important in the life of the Empire, dedicated not only to religion but also to justice

Like the burgeoning Roman Empire itself, the city's uncovered remains continue to grow, even into the third millennium when this fine museum opened and more of the surrounding area was excavated.

Trajan's Markets The Mercati di Traiano were originally thought to have been the precursor of modern shopping malls—a group of commercial buildings constructed in the second century AD as a semicircular range of halls on three levels. Two of the levels survive in excellent condition. But it's now thought the 'markets' were probably a new hub for politics and justice inaugurated by the Emperor Trajan in AD112 before his death in AD117, and the 150 or so booths and halls of the structure were offices once populated by civil servants, though some

Clockwise from far left: The large complex known as Trajan's Markets, where Romans gathered to conduct business; a lone column by the 13th-century Torre delle Milizie; statues on display in one of the ancient streets; carved reliefs on Trajan's Column recall the emperor's battles

at ground level may have been shops. Either way, they present a magnificent spectacle.

Museum The labyrinthine museum within Trajan's Markets is an absorbing peep into Rome's distant past. Opened in 2007, it presents the grand Imperial Fora using modern techniques, including film and pictographic illustration, as well as items unearthed in recent excavations in the area. The external viewing gallery gives a splendid view, not only of the surrounding ruins, but the whole Forums area of ancient Rome, as well as the AD113 Trajan's Column, which stands at 30m (100ft), built of hollow marble. Additionally, since 2008, the Museo dei Fori Imperiali has been a venue for contemporary arts, with regular displays of paintings and specially convened exhibitions.

THE BASICS

www.mercatiditraiano.it

➕ H6

✉ Via IV Novembre 94

☎ 06 0608; online tickets www.omniticket.it

🕐 Tue–Sun 9–7 (last admission 1 hour before closing)

🚇 Cavour

🚌 H, 40, 64, 70, 117, 170 and other routes to Via IV Novembre

♿ Good

💶 Expensive

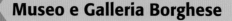

HIGHLIGHT

● Antonio Canova's sculpture of Paolina Borghese (1804), who was Napoleon's sister and the wife of Camillo Borghese. She is shown bare-breasted and looks every bit as seductive in marble as she was in real life

The Galleria Borghese may be small, but what it lacks in quantity it more than makes up for in quality. The gallery combines paintings and sculptures, including many masterpieces by Gian Lorenzo Bernini, Raphael, Caravaggio and others.

Bernini sculptures The Villa Borghese was designed in 1613 as a summer retreat for Cardinal Scipione Borghese, nephew of Pope Paul V, who accumulated most of the collection (acquired by the state in 1902). Scipione was an enthusiastic patron of Bernini, whose works dominate one floor of the gallery. His *David* (1623–24) is said to be a self-portrait, while *Apollo and Daphne* (1622–25), in the next room, is considered his masterpiece. Other Bernini works include the *Rape of Proserpina*

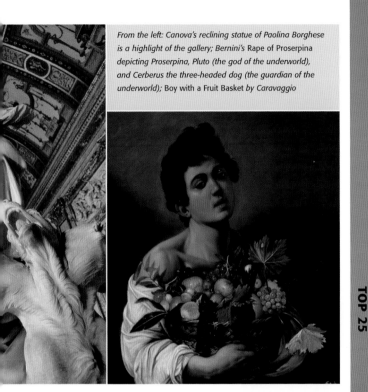

From the left: Canova's reclining statue of Paolina Borghese is a highlight of the gallery; Bernini's *Rape of Proserpina* depicting Proserpina, Pluto (the god of the underworld), and Cerberus the three-headed dog (the guardian of the underworld); Boy with a Fruit Basket *by Caravaggio*

(1622) and *Truth Unveiled by Time* (1652). The statues are complemented by some of Rome's most beautifully decorated rooms.

The setting The museum, in the grounds of the Villa Borghese, (▷ 75), north of the city, is Rome's largest public park—200 acres (80ha) with five museums, gardens, lakes, fountains and a deer park. Before Cardinal Scipione made the grounds the base of his 17th-century pleasure palace, they were vineyards.

The paintings Foremost in this wonderful collection are works by Raphael *(The Deposition of Christ*, 1507), Titian *(Sacred and Profane Love*, 1512), Caravaggio *(Boy with a Fruit Basket* and *Madonna dei Palafrenieri*, 1605) and Correggio *(Danae*, 1530).

THE BASICS

www.galleriaborghese.it

➕ J2

✉ Piazzale del Museo Borghese 5

☎ 06 841 3979; obligatory reservations 06 32810; www.tosc.it

🕐 Tue–Sun 8.30–7.30; closed public holidays

🚇 Spagna or Flaminio

🚌 116 to Viale del Museo Borghese, or 52, 53, 910 to Via Pinciana or C3, 19 to Via delle Belle Arti

♿ Steps to front entrance

💶 Expensive

HIGHLIGHTS

● The Museum
● Piazzale della Corporazione
● The Baths of Neptune
● Casa di Diana

TIPS

● Allow a whole day for the site; perhaps bring a picnic.
● In summer, take water with you and rest in the shade during the early afternoon.
● Buy a plan of the site and spend time when you arrive planning your visit.

Imperial Rome's port is one of the three best-preserved ancient towns in Italy. More than an historical treasury, Ostia's ruins invoke an intense visual sense of the past.

Living history Less celebrated than Pompeii or Herculaneum, Ostia Antica more than rivals its sisters. Lying 25km (15 miles) southwest of Rome, its 4,049ha (10,000-acre) pastoral setting would do justice to Italy's most glorious countryside. Located on the Tiber, the port town was Rome's trade link with the outside world for 600 years—until a receding coastline and imperial decline hastened its demise. By the 17th century Ostia was all but forgotten. Legend claims its foundation in the Etruscan seventh century BC—but archaeological dating places it in the Roman fourth century BC.

Left: Detail of the remains of a Corinthian capital, preserved from the ruins and displayed at the archaeological site; below: The fine remnants, including the amphitheatre, at this well-preserved Roman town give a good impression of what everyday life was like in an ancient port city

The site What we see today is only about half of the town, uncovered by archaeological excavations that began in the 19th century, and which continue today. Pride of place goes to the vast 4,000-seat amphitheatre that is still used for open-air concerts in the summer. There are remarkable discoveries all along and leading off from the main road, Decumanus Maximus, which is rutted where laden carts once carried goods to and from the great port. Set in luxuriant greenery and surrounded by Aleppo pines and cedars, are the remains of the Forum, a second-century AD multi-storey apartment block called the Casa di Diana, the Baths of Neptune with its splendid mosaics, and the Piazzale della Corporazione, the original business district, which is flanked by the remains of shops, offices and *horrea* (warehouses).

THE BASICS

http://archeoroma.
beniculturali.it
✚ Off map
✉ Viale dei Romagnoli
717
☎ 06 5635 8099
◷ Apr–Oct Tue–Sun
8.30–7.30 (last admission
6); Nov–Feb 8.30–5 (last
admission 4); Mar 8.30–6
(last admission 5); closed
public holidays
🍴 Restaurant
🚇 Metro line B to
Piramide, then train from
adjoining Roma–Lido
station (covered by BIG
ticket, ▷ 167)
🎟 Moderate

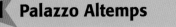

HIGHLIGHTS

● Aphrodite's throne
● *Galatian Soldier* statue
● Courtyard loggia
● Statue of Orestes and Electra embracing in a fond farewell

TIP

● The Palazzo Altemps is easily seen in conjunction with Piazza Navona. But note that its sister museum, the Palazzo Massimo alle Terme, is a long way away, by Termini Station.

This beautiful building epitomizes the best of Renaissance urban architecture, while its elegant rooms provide the setting for some of the finest of Rome's Classical sculpture.

The building Rome's Museo Nazionale Romano (National Roman Museum) is housed in two superbly restored buildings: the Palazzo Massimo alle Terme (▷ 40–41) near the station and here in the Palazzo Altemps, whose odd-sounding name is the Italian corruption of the German name von Hohenemps. Mainly constructed in the 15th century, the building houses a series of charming and intimate rooms, many with vaulted ceilings. One gives access to a splendidly frescoed loggia overlooking the comings and goings of a harmonious inner courtyard. The best time to get a sense of

Clockwise from far left: The statue of Orestes and Electra; elegant rooms provide a stunning backdrop for the collections; the Ludovisi Throne shows Aphrodite being plucked from the sea; statues watch over the Palazzo Altemps' peaceful inner courtyard

the building's history is as dusk falls, when the rooms and exhibits are imaginatively lit.

The collections The palazzo is home to the famous Ludovisi Collection, amassed by Cardinal Ludovico Ludovisi in the 17th century, as well as the Altemps collection of Egyptian antiques and portraits. Downstairs look for the *Tiber Apollo*, found in the bed of the river in the late 19th century, and the two gigantic statues of Athena. Upstairs, the star of the collection, the Ludovisi Throne, is probably a Greek sculpture dedicated as a throne for Aphrodite. From the fifth century BC, the delicate carving portrays the goddess rising from the sea foam. Do not miss the statue of the *Galatian Soldier and His Wife Committing Suicide,* apparently commissioned by Julius Caesar.

THE BASICS

http://archeoroma.
beniculturali.it

➕ F5

✉ Via di Sant'Apollinare 8

☎ 06 687 2719 (ticket office) or 06 3996 7700; book online at www.coopculture.it

🕐 Tue–Sun 9–7.45

🚌 30, 70, 87, 116, 492 to Corso del Rinascimento

♿ Moderate; combined ticket with Palazzo Massimo alle Terme, Crypta Balbi and Terme di Diocleziano

HIGHLIGHTS

- Scala Elicoidale
- *Madonna and Child* and *Annunciation*, Filippo Lippi
- *Holy Family* and *Madonna and Saints*, Andrea del Sarto
- *Madonna and Child*, Beccafumi
- Borromini's false-perspective window on the top floor
- *Adoration of the Shepherds* and *Baptism of Christ*, El Greco
- *Judith and Holofernes* and *Narciso*, Caravaggio
- *Beatrice Cenci*, attributed to Guido Reni
- *Henry VIII*, attributed to Holbein
- *The Triumph of Divine Providence*, Pietro da Cortona (Gran Salone)

The magnificent Palazzo Barberini—designed by Bernini, Borromini and Carlo Maderno—houses a stupendous ceiling fresco and one of Rome's finest art collections, the Galleria Nazionale d'Arte Antica.

Urban's grandeur The palace was commissioned by Maffeo Barberini for his family when he became Pope Urban VIII in 1623. It was begun by Carlo Maderno and completed by Bernini. The epitome of Rome's high baroque style, it is a maze of sumptuous suites, apartments and staircases. Overshadowing all is the Gran Salone, dominated by Pietro da Cortona's rich ceiling frescoes (1639), glorifying Urban as an agent of Divine Providence. The central windows and oval spiral staircase (Scala Elicoidale) are the work of Borromini.

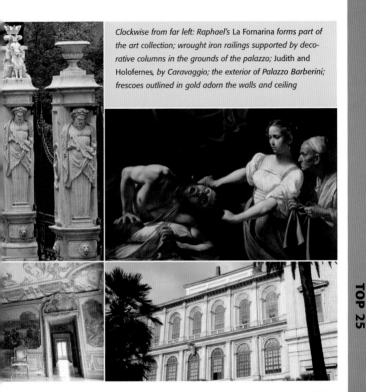

Clockwise from far left: Raphael's La Fornarina forms part of the art collection; wrought iron railings supported by decorative columns in the grounds of the palazzo; Judith and Holofernes, by Caravaggio; the exterior of Palazzo Barberini; frescoes outlined in gold adorn the walls and ceiling

The collection 'Antica' here means old rather than ancient. Probably the most popular painting in the collection is Raphael's *La Fornarina* (also attributed to Giulio Romano). It is reputedly a portrait of one of the artist's several mistresses, identified later as the daughter of a *fornaio* (baker). It was executed in the year of the painter's death, a demise brought on, it is said, by his mistress's unrelenting passion. Elsewhere, eminent Italian works from Filippo Lippi, Andrea del Sarto, Caravaggio and Guido Reni stand alongside paintings by leading foreign artists, such as El Greco (a Nativity and the *Baptism of Christ*) and Holbein (a portrait of Henry VIII, dressed for his wedding to Anne of Cleves). Also here is a splendid collection of furniture, ceramics and other beautiful decorative arts.

THE BASICS

www.galleriaborghese.it/
barberini
⊞ J4
⊠ Via delle Quattro
Fontane 13
☎ 06 482 4184 or 06
32810; online www.tosc.it
🕓 Tue–Sun 8.30–7.30
🚇 Barberini
🚌 52, 53, 61, 62, 63, 71,
80, 95, 116, 119 to Via del
Tritone or H, 40, 60, 64,
70, 71, 170 to Via
Nazionale
♿ Few
💶 Moderate

HIGHLIGHTS

● *Religion Succoured by Spain* (tagged 10), Titian
● *Portrait of Two Venetians* (23), Raphael
● *Maddalena* (40) and *Rest on the Flight into Egypt* (42), Caravaggio
● *Birth* and *Marriage of the Virgin* (174/176), Giovanni di Paolo
● *Nativity* (200), Parmigianino
● *Salomé with Head of John the Baptist*, Titian
● *Innocent X*, Bernini
● *Battle of the Bay of Naples* (317), Pieter Brueghel the Elder
● *Penitant Magdalen*, Caravaggio

TIPS

● Use the audioguide, which is included in the price and helps make sense of what you're seeing.
● The paintings are not well lit so it is better to visit during daylight hours.

This is one of Rome's largest palaces and contains one of the city's finest patrician art collections. It also offers the chance to admire some of the sumptuously decorated rooms of its private apartments.

A dynasty Little in the bland exterior of the Palazzo Doria Pamphilj prepares you for the glory of the beautiful rooms that lie within. The core of the building was erected in 1435, and it has withstood countless alterations and owners. The Doria Pamphilj dynasty was formed by yoking together the Doria, a famous Genoese seafaring clan, and the Pamphilj, a noble Roman family. Most people come here for the paintings, but—when open—you can also enjoy a guided tour around some of the private apartments in the 1,000-room palace. The most

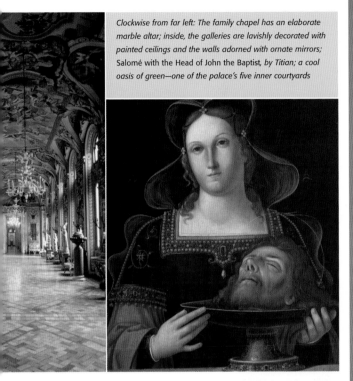

Clockwise from far left: The family chapel has an elaborate marble altar; inside, the galleries are lavishly decorated with painted ceilings and the walls adorned with ornate mirrors; Salomé with the Head of John the Baptist, by Titian; a cool oasis of green—one of the palace's five inner courtyards

impressive is the Saletta Gialla (Yellow Room), decorated with 12 Gobelin tapestries made for Louis XV. In the Salone Verde (Green Room) are three important paintings: an Annunciation by Filippo Lippi, *Portrait of a Gentleman* by Lorenzo Lotto and *Andrea Doria* (a famous admiral) by Sebastiano del Piombo.

Labyrinth of masterpieces The Pamphilj's art collection is displayed in ranks in four broad galleries. As the works are numbered, not tagged, it's worth investing in a guidebook from the ticket office. The finest painting is the famous Velázquez portrait, *Innocent X* (1650), a likeness that captured the pope's weak and suspicious nature so adroitly that Innocent is said to have lamented that it was 'too true, too true'.

THE BASICS

www.dopart.it

⊞ G5

✉ Via del Corso 305

☎ 06 679 7323

🕐 Daily 9–7; plus evening concerts (expensive) when gallery can be viewed

🍴 Café-bar on ground floor

🚌 60, 62, 85, 95, 160, 492 and all other services to Piazza Venezia

♿ Good

💰 Gallery expensive. Apartments moderate

HIGHLIGHTS

● *Niobid from the Hortus Sallustiani* (Room VIII)
● The collection of coins in the basement
● *The Sleeping Hermaphrodite* (Room VII)
● House of Livia (Room II)
● The Villa Farnesina (Gallery II, Rooms III–V)

TIP

● The combined ticket is also valid for all parts of the Museo Nazionale Romano, notably the Palazzo Altemps.

This sublime collection of Greek and Roman sculpture, with outstanding and unique displays of ancient Roman wall paintings and mosaics, dates from the end of the Republican age to the late Imperial age.

The building The Palazzo Massimo is an elegant and airy palace, beautifully renovated for the millennium. The palace, designed by Camillo Pistrucci, was built in the late 19th century by the Massimo family to replace an earlier one demolished to make way for Termini station. In 1981 the palace was acquired by the state, and in the 1990s it was transformed into one of Rome's most attractive museums. The palace has four floors of museum space, a modern library, a conference room and a computer-based documentation area.

Clockwise from far left: A pavement mosaic of the head of Pan forms part of the outstanding displays; a fourth-century BC marble inlay panel; the Lancellotti Discobolus (Discus Thrower) is among the masterpieces in the collection; intricate patterns frame this third-century BC mosaic of Dionysus

The collection One of the two buildings (the other being the Palazzo Altemps, ▷ 34–35) housing Rome's magnificent Classical collections. Here you'll find some of Rome's greatest treasures, ranging from naked gods and games players to sarcophagi and goddesses. Don't miss the portrait busts or the wonderful Roman frescoes and mosaics on the upper floor.

Lancellotti Discobolus This fine marble copy of the great *Discus Thrower* dates from the mid-second century AD, and is one of the most famous copies of a fifth-century BC work. Discovered in the 18th century, it was sent to Germany during World War II and returned in 1948. It reproduces an original bronze that was probably the work of Myron, a Greek sculptor renowned for his portraits of athletes.

THE BASICS

http://archeoroma.beniculturali.it

+ K5

✉ Piazza dei Cinquecento 67–Largo di Villa Peretti 1

☎ Reservations 06 3996 7700 or online at www.coopculture.it

🕐 Tue–Sun 9–7.45

🚇 Termini or Repubblica

🚌 All services to Termini and Piazza dei Cinquecento

♿ Moderate; combined ticket with Palazzo Altemps, Crypta Balbi and Terme di Diocleziano

HIGHLIGHTS

● Facade inscription
● Pedimented portico
● Original Roman doors
● Marble interior and pavement
● Coffered dome and *oculus*
● Tomb of Raphael
● Royal tombs

TIP

● The Pantheon is often very crowded. To make the most of your visit, go on a weekday or early in the morning.

No other monument suggests the grandeur of ancient Rome as magnificently as this temple, whose early conversion to a place of Christian worship has rendered it the most perfect of the city's ancient monuments.

Temple and church The greatest surviving complete Roman structure, built by Emperor Hadrian in AD118–28, the Pantheon replaced a temple of 27BC by Marcus Agrippa, son-in-law of Augustus. (Modestly, Hadrian retained the original inscription proclaiming it as Agrippa's work.) It became the church of Santa Maria ad Martyres in AD609 (the bones of martyrs were brought here from the Catacombs) and is now a shrine to Italy's 'immortals', including the artist Raphael and kings Vittore Emanuele II and Umberto I.

Clockwise from far left: Visitors gaze in astonishment at the interior where massive Egyptian granite columns support the dome; the sun pours in through the oculus, an opening in the Pantheon's roof; the Pantheon borders Piazza della Rotonda and fountain by Giacomo della Porta

An engineering marvel Massive and simple from the outside, the Pantheon is at its most breathtaking inside, where the scale, harmony and symmetry of the dome in particular are more apparent. The world's largest dome until 1882 (when it was surpassed in the English spa resort of Buxton), it has a diameter of 43.3m (142ft)—equal to its height from the floor. Weight and stresses were reduced by rows of coffers in the ceiling, and the use of progressively lighter materials from the base to the crown. The central *oculus*, 9m (30ft) in diameter and clearly intended to inspire meditation on the heavens above, lets light (and rain) fall onto the marble pavement far below. Relax in one of Piazza della Rotonda's cafés to enjoy and admire the exterior view of the Pantheon and the atmosphere of the piazza.

THE BASICS

🗺 F5
✉ Piazza della Rotonda
☎ 06 6830 0230
🕐 Mon–Sat 8.30–7.30, Sun 9–6, public holidays 9–1
🚌 116, 119 to Piazza della Rotonda or 40, 64, 70 and all other services to Largo di Torre Argentina
♿ Good
✋ Free

HIGHLIGHTS

- Street market
- Wine bar Vineria Reggio (▷ 137)
- Statue of Giordano Bruno marking where the philosopher was martyred for heresy in 1600
- Piazza della Cancelleria
- Palazzo Pio Righetti
- Santa Maria dell'Orazione e Morte: church door decorated with stone skulls
- The inscription on 'new' La Terrina (Tureen) fountain: 'Do well and let them talk'

There is nowhere more relaxing in Rome to sit and watch the world go by than Campo de' Fiori, a lovely old piazza whose fruit, vegetable and fish market makes it one of the liveliest and most vivid corners of the old city.

Ancient square Piazza Campo de' Fiori, or the 'Field of Flowers', was turned in the Middle Ages from a meadow facing the ancient Theatre of Pompey (55BC; now the Palazzo Pio Righetti) into one of the city's most exclusive residential and business districts. By the 15th century it was surrounded by busy inns and bordellos, some run by the infamous courtesan Vannozza Catanei, mistress of the Borgia pope Alexander VI. By 1600 it had also become a place of execution, the fate of Giordano Bruno, a

Clockwise from far left: A selection of squashes for sale at the market; at night the bars and cafés are popular meeting places; a string of red chillies adorns a market stall; crates of fresh fruit and vegetables are transported around the market; stalls display their colourful produce

Dominican priest and philospher whose cowled statue stands at the centre of the piazza.

Present day Just sit back and soak up the atmosphere. Students, foreigners, locals and tramps mingle with market vendors shouting their wares, while the cafés, bars and the wonderfully atmospheric wine bar at No. 15, the Vineria Reggio, will have you relishing the street life. One block south lies Piazza Farnese, dominated by the Palazzo Farnese, a Renaissance masterpiece partly designed by Michelangelo and begun in 1516. It is now home to the French Embassy. One block west is the Palazzo della Cancelleria (1485), once the papal chancellery. The nearby Via Giulia, Via dei Baullari, the busy Via dei Cappellari and Via del Pellegrino are all wonderful streets to explore.

THE BASICS

➕ F6

✉ Piazza Campo de' Fiori

🕐 Market Mon–Sat 7–1.30

🚌 40, 46, 62, 64 to Corso Vittorio Emanuele II or H, 8, 46, 62, 64, 70, 87 to Largo di Torre Argentina

♿ Cobbled streets and some kerbs around piazza

🆓 Free

HIGHLIGHTS

- Fontana dei Quattro Fiumi (centre)
- Fontana del Moro (south)
- Fontana del Nettuno (north)
- Palazzo Pamphilj
- San Luigi dei Francesi (Via Santa Giovanna d'Arco)
- Santa Maria dell'Anima (Via della Pace)

Piazza di Spagna may be more elegant and Campo de' Fiori more vivid, but Piazza Navona, with its atmospheric echoes of a 2,000-year history, is a glorious place to amble or stop for a drink at a sun-drenched table and watch the world go by.

Shaping history Piazza Navona owes its unmistakable elliptical shape to a stadium and racetrack built here in AD86 by Emperor Domitian. From the Circus Agonalis—the stadium for athletic games—comes the piazza's present name, rendered in medieval Latin as *in agone*, and then in Rome's strangulated dialect as *'n 'agona*. The stadium was used until well into the Middle Ages for festivals and competitions. The square owes its present appearance to its rebuilding by Pope Innocent X in 1644.

Clockwise from far left: Bernini's Fontana dei Quattro Fiumi is the largest fountain in Piazza Navona; the piazza at night; sculptural detail on the Fontana dei Quattro Fiumi; elegant cafés and restaurants line the square; passing the time of day beside the Fontana del Moro in the north of the square

Around the piazza Bernini's spirited Fontana dei Quattro Fiumi (Fountain of the Four Rivers), dominates. Unveiled in 1651, it has four figures that represent the four rivers of Paradise (the Nile, Ganges, Danube and Plate), and the four 'corners' of the world (Africa, Asia, Europe and America). On the west side of the piazza is the baroque Sant' Agnese in Agone (1652–57), its facade designed by Borromini. Bernini's river gods are said to recoil in horror from his rival's work. Beside it stands the Palazzo Pamphilj, commissioned by Innocent X and now the Brazilian Embassy. Further afield, San Luigi dei Francesi is famous for three superlative Caravaggio paintings (in the rear chapel of the left nave), and Santa Maria della Pace for a cloister by Bramante and Raphael's frescoes of the four *Sybils*.

THE BASICS

✚ F5
✉ Piazza Navona
🚇 Spagna
🚌 30, 70, 87, 116, 492, 628 to Corso del Rinascimento or 40, 46, 62, 64 to Corso Vittorio Emanuele II

Neither old nor particularly striking, the Spanish Steps are one of Rome's most popular meeting points, thanks largely to their views, at the heart of Piazza di Spagna in the city's exclusive shopping district.

Spanish Steps Despite their name, the Spanish Steps were commissioned by French ambassador Étienne Gueffier, who in 1723 sought to link Piazza di Spagna with the French-owned church of Trinità dei Monti on the hill above. A century earlier the piazza had housed the headquarters of the Spanish ambassador to the Holy See, hence the name of the steps and the square.

Around the steps At the base of the steps is the Fontana della Barcaccia, commissioned in

Left: From Piazza di Spagna the monumental staircase known as the Spanish Steps rises towards the beautiful Trinità dei Monti with its Gothic facade and twin bell towers; below: The Fontana della Barcaccia, at the foot of the steps, was designed by Bernini in the shape of a small boat

1627 by Pope Urban VIII and designed either by Gian Lorenzo Bernini or by his less famous father, Pietro. The eccentric design represents a half-sunken boat. As you face the steps from below, to your right stands the Museo Keats-Shelley (▷ 70), with its fascinating collection of literary memorabilia and a working library housed in the lodgings where the poet John Keats died in 1821, aged 25. At the top of the steps you can enjoy views past the magnificent Palazzo Barberini (▷ 36–37) and towards the Quirinal Hill; walk into the simple Trinità dei Monti church, with its double exterior stairs by Domenico Fontana; and visit the beautiful gardens of the 16th-century Villa Medici, the seat of the French Academy in Rome, where French scholars come to study painting, sculpture, architecture, engraving and music.

THE BASICS

➕ G4
✉ Piazza di Spagna
☎ Villa Medici 06 67611; www.villamedici.it. Trinità dei Monti 06 679 4179
🕐 Spanish Steps always open. Trinità dei Monti 6.30am–8pm. Villa Medici guided visits Tue–Sun at 11, 2/2.30, 3, 4/4.30 plus 6 Jun–Aug in Italian and French. In English at noon
🍴 Babington's Tea Rooms
🚇 Spagna
🚌 117, 119 to Piazza di Spagna
♿ None for Spanish Steps
🎟 Free

HIGHLIGHTS

● Choir screen
● Chapel of St.
Catherine: fresco cycle
● *Ciborio* (altar canopy)
● Apse mosaic: *The Triumph of the Cross*
● Monument to Cardinal Roverella, Giovanni Dalmata (upper church)
● Fresco: *Miracle of San Clemente* (upper church)
● Fresco: *Legend of Sisinnio* (lower church)
● *Triclinium*
● Altar of Mithras: bas-relief of Mithras slaying the bull

No site in Rome reveals as vividly the layers of history that underpin the city as this beautiful medieval ensemble, built over a superbly preserved fourth-century church and the atmospheric remains of a third-century Roman Mithraic temple.

The upper church The present San Clemente, which was named after Rome's fourth pope, was built between 1108 and 1184 to replace an earlier church that was sacked by the Normans in 1084. Almost untouched since, its medieval interior is dominated by the 12th-century marble panels of the choir screen and pulpits and the glittering 12th-century apse mosaic, *The Triumph of the Cross*. Equally captivating are the *Life of St. Catherine* frescoes (1428–31) by Masolino da Panicale.

Clockwise from far left: The 12th-century choir and altar in the upper church; exploring the excavated levels below the present church; detail of Masolino's Crucifixion fresco; the plain exterior of San Clemente; the decorated altar of Mithras is flanked by stone benches

Below ground Steps descend to the lower church, which retains traces of 8th- to 11th-century frescoes of San Clemente and the legends of St. Alessio and St. Sisinnio. More steps lead deeper into the twilight world of the best-preserved of the 12 Mithraic temples uncovered in Rome. (Mithraism was a popular, men-only cult that orginated in Persia – modern day Iran – but was later eclipsed by Christianity.) Here are an altar with a bas-relief of Mithras ritually slaying a bull, and the *triclinium*, used for banquets and rites. Ongoing excavations are revealing parts of the temple, the Mithraic schoolroom, and the 1,900-year-old remains of buildings, alleyways and streets. Even today you can hear an underground stream, which may have formed part of ancient Rome's drainage system.

THE BASICS

www.basilicasanclemente.com

➕ K7

✉ Via di San Giovanni in Laterano (corner of Via Labicana)

☎ 06 774 0021

🕐 Mon–Sat 9–12.30, 3–6, Sun excavations 12–6

🚇 Colosseo

🚌 60, 85, 87, 117, 175 to Piazza del Colosseo or 85, 117, 850 to Via di San Giovanni in Laterano

♿ Church free; excavations moderate

HIGHLIGHTS

● The world's oldest icon of the Virgin Mary, said to be 1,000 years old, in the Pauline Chapel

● Bernini's painting, *St. Cajetan Holding The Holy Child*

● The Crypt of the Nativity, with the tombs of many eminent men of the church

Santa Maria Maggiore is rightly considered Rome's finest Early Christian basilica, thanks to its majestic interior and many magnificent mosaics.

History According to a myth, the Virgin appeared to Pope Liberius on 5 August AD352, and told him to build a church exactly where snow would fall the next day. Although it was summer, snow fell, marking the outlines of a basilica on the Esquiline Hill. Legend aside, the church probably dates from AD430, though the campanile (the tallest in Rome at 75m/246ft) was added in 1377 and the interior and exterior were substantially altered in the 13th and 18th centuries. The coffered ceiling, attributed to Giuliano da Sangallo, was reputedly gilded with the first gold to arrive from the New World,

Clockwise from far left: Santa Maria Maggiore's amazing gilded ceiling; Ferdinando Fuga's 18th-century facade and the 14th-century campanile; mosaic detail of the Coronation of the Virgin with Saints and Angels; the decorated dome of the Cappella Paolina, on the left-hand side of the nave

a gift from Spain to Pope Alexander VI (note his Borgia bull emblems).

Rich decoration Beyond the general grandeur, the main treasures are the 36 mosaics in the architraves of the nave, fifth-century depictions of the lives of Moses, Abraham, Isaac and Jacob, framed by some 40 ancient columns. Also compelling are the mosaics in the loggia and on the triumphal arch. In the 13th-century apse are mosaics by Jacopo Torriti, the pinnacle of Rome's medieval mosaic tradition. Other highlights include the Cappella Sistina (tomb of Pope Sixtus V) by Domenico Fontana (1588); the Cappella Paolina, built by Paul V (1611); and Giovanni di Cosma's tomb of Cardinal Rodriguez (1299). The high altar reputedly contains a relic of Christ's crib.

THE BASICS

www.vatican.va

☐ K5

✉ Piazza di Santa Maria Maggiore and Piazza dell'Esquilino

☎ 06 6988 6800

🕐 Daily 7–6.45
Loggia: guided tours Mar–Oct daily 9–6.30; Nov–Feb 9–1

🚇 Termini or Cavour

🚌 C3, 16, 70, 71, 75, 84, 360 to Piazza di Santa Maria Maggiore

♿ Poor: access is easiest from Piazza di Santa Maria Maggiore

💶 Church free; Loggia and museum inexpensive

HIGHLIGHTS

● Plaques on the side of the building marking the height of the Tiber floods, which plagued the city between 1422 and 1870
● The church's star-spangled blue ceiling
● Relics of St. Catherine of Siena, and preserved room in sacristy where she died
● The headquarters of the Dominican preaching order, which serves the church, to the left of the building
● The sixth-century BC Egyptian obelisk above Bernini's elephant, known as Pulcino della Minerva (Minerva's chick)

Remarkable in having retained many Gothic features despite Rome's love for the baroque, behind its plain facade Santa Maria sopra Minerva is a cornucopia of tombs, paintings and Renaissance sculpture.

Florentine influences Originally founded in the eighth century over ruins of a temple to Roman goddess Minerva, the church was built in 1280 to a design by two Florentine Dominican monks who fashioned it on their own church, Santa Maria Novella. Before entering the church, notice its strange but charming statue of an elephant supporting a sixth-century BC Egyptian obelisk in the pretty piazza outside. It was designed by Bernini in the 17th century. The elephant was chosen as an ancient symbol of piety and wisdom.

Clockwise from far left: Bernini's elephant supports an Egyptian obelisk in the piazza; the soaring Gothic arched ceiling painted blue with gold stars; the elaborate tomb of St. Catherine of Siena lies beneath the high altar; the aisles and side chapels are filled with tombs and works of art

Inside The interior of the church abounds with beautiful works, such as the Cappella Carafa (whose fine porch is attributed to Giuliano da Maiano) and Michelangelo's calm statue *The Risen Christ* (1521), left of the high altar. Filippino Lippi painted the celebrated frescoes of *St. Thomas Aquinas* and the *Assumption* (1488–93). Among other sculptures are the tombs of Francesco Tornabuoni (1480) and that of Giovanni Alberini, the latter decorated with reliefs of Hercules (15th century). Both are attributed to Mino da Fiesole. Other works include Fra Angelico's tomb slab (1455); the tombs of Medici popes Clement VII and Leo X (1536) by Antonio da Sangallo the Younger; and Bernini's monument to Maria Raggi (1643). St. Catherine of Siena, one of Italy's patron saints, is buried beneath the high altar.

THE BASICS

✚ G5

✉ Piazza della Minerva 42

☎ 06 679 3926

🕐 Mon–Sat 7.10–7, Sun 8–12, 2–7

🚌 H, 8, 30, 40, 46, 62, 64, 70, 81, 87 to Largo di Torre Argentina or 119 to Piazza della Rotonda

♿ Stepped access to church

🎫 Free

TOP 25

HIGHLIGHTS

- Cappella Costa, with the tombs of Giovanni Borgia, son of Pope Alexander VI (1492–1503), and his mother Vannozza Cattenei
- *Coronation of the Virgin*, Pinturicchio
- Tombs of cardinals Ascanio Sforza and Girolamo Basso della Rovere
- Fresco: *Life of San Girolamo*, Tiberio d'Assisi
- *Delphic Sybil*, Pinturicchio
- Altar, Andrea Bregno
- The oldest stained-glass windows in Rome

Santa Maria del Popolo's appeal stems from its intimate size and location, and from a wonderfully varied and rich collection of works of art ranging from masterpieces by Caravaggio to some of Rome's earliest stained-glass windows.

Renaissance achievement Founded in 1099 on the site of Nero's grave, Santa Maria del Popolo was rebuilt by Pope Sixtus IV in 1472 and extended later by Bramante and Bernini. The right nave's first chapel, the Cappella della Rovere, is decorated with frescoes on the *Life of San Girolamo* (1485–90) by Tiberio d'Assisi, a pupil of Pinturicchio whose *Nativity* (c.1490) graces the chapel's main altar. The apse contains two fine stained-glass windows (1509) by the French artist Guillaume de Marcillat.

Clockwise from far left: Carracci's Assumption of the Virgin is the altarpiece of the Cappella Cerasi (Cerasi Chapel); Caravaggio's Crucifixion of St. Peter; the baroque facade of Santa Maria del Popolo; looking towards the richly decorated high altar

On either side are the greatest of the church's monuments: the tombs of the cardinals Ascanio Sforza (1505, left) and Girolamo Basso della Rovere (1507, right). Both are the work of Andrea Sansovino. High on the walls are superb and elegant frescoes (1508–10) of the *Virgin*, *Evangelists*, the *Fathers of the Church* and *Sybils* by Pinturicchio.

North nave The first chapel of the left transept, the Cappella Cerasi, contains three major paintings: the altarpiece, an *Assumption of the Virgin* by Annibale Carracci; and Caravaggio's dramatic *Conversion of St. Paul* and the *Crucifixion of St. Peter* (all 1601). The famous Cappella Chigi (1513), the second chapel in the north aisle, was commissioned by the Sienese banker Agostino Chigi from Raphael and Bernini.

THE BASICS

www.santamariadel popolo.it

+ F2

✉ Piazza del Popolo 12

☎ 06 361 0836

🕐 Mon–Sat 7–12, 4–7, Sun 7.30–1.30, 4.30–7.30

Ⓜ Flaminio

🚌 117, 119 to Piazza del Popolo

♿ Few

🆓 Free

HIGHLIGHTS

- Romanesque campanile
- Facade mosaics
- Portico
- Ceiling, by Domenichino
- Cosmati marble pavement
- Wall tabernacle by Mino del Reame (central nave)
- Byzantine gold mosaics in upper and lower apse
- The nave's Roman columns; some from the Terme di Caracalla
- Madonna della Clemenza in the Cappella Altemps
- Cappella Avila: baroque chapel

TIP

- Visit in the evening, then have a drink in one of the outdoor cafés, from where you can appreciate the lit piazza and basilica.

One of the most memorable sights of night-time Rome is the 12th-century gold mosaics on the facade of Santa Maria in Trastevere, their floodlit glow casting a gentle light over the piazza below.

Early church Santa Maria in Trastevere is among the oldest officially sanctioned places of worship in Rome. It was founded in around AD222, allegedly on the spot where a fountain of olive oil had sprung from the earth on the day of Christ's birth (symbolizing the coming of the grace of God). Much of the present church was built in the 12th century during the reign of Innocent II. Inside, the main colonnade of the nave is composed of reused and ancient Roman columns. The portico, containing frag-ments of Roman reliefs and inscriptions, and

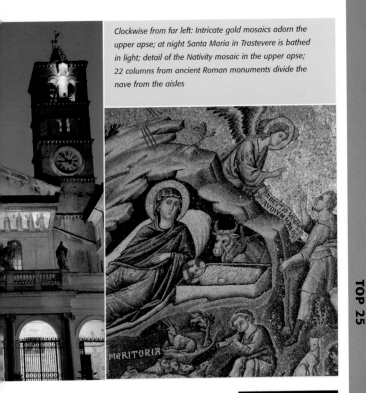

Clockwise from far left: Intricate gold mosaics adorn the upper apse; at night Santa Maria in Trastevere is bathed in light; detail of the Nativity mosaic in the upper apse; 22 columns from ancient Roman monuments divide the nave from the aisles

MERITORIA

medieval remains, was added in 1702 by Carlo Fontana, who was responsible for the fountain that graces the adjoining piazza.

Mosaics The facade mosaics probably date from the mid-12th century, and depict the Virgin and Child with 10 lamp-carrying companions. Long believed to portray the parable of the Wise and Foolish Virgins, their subject matter is contested, as several 'virgins' appear to be men and only two are carrying unlighted lamps (not the five of the parable). The mosaics of the upper apse inside the church, devoted to the glorification of the Virgin, date from the same period and are Byzantine-influenced works by Greek or Greek-trained craftsmen. Those below, depicting scenes from the life of the Virgin (1291), are by the mosaicist and fresco painter Pietro Cavallini.

THE BASICS

✚ E7

✉ Piazza Santa Maria in Trastevere

☎ 06 581 9443

🕐 Daily 7.30am–9pm (may close 12.30–3.30 in winter)

🚌 H, 8 to Viale di Trastevere, 125 to Via Manara or 23, 280 to Lungotevere Raffaello Sanzio

♿ Wheelchair accessible

🆓 Free

HIGHLIGHTS

● Peruzzi's vibrant frescoes of *trompe l'oeil* views of Rome in the Sala delle Prospettive
● The gardens
● Raphael's fresco *Trionfo di Galatea (Triumph of Galatea)*

TIP

● Within the building is also the National Print Collection (Gabinetto Nazionale delle Stampe), part of the National Institute of Graphics, which can be visited by permission.

This is one of the most intimate and charming of all Rome's grand houses, known as much for its peaceful gardens as for its beautifully decorated interior, which contains works commissioned from Raphael and other artists by the villa's original owner, Agostino Chigi.

All to impress In 1508 Agostino Chigi, a wealthy banker from Siena, commissioned Baldasssare Peruzzi to build him a suburban villa. Here, Chigi entertained artists, princes and cardinals. His banquets were memorable: after the meal, it is said that Chigi would have the gold and silver dishes thrown into the Tiber to impress his guests with his wealth. What they did not know was that the plates were caught by safety nets and returned to the kitchens.

Clockwise from far left: Visitors on a guided tour in the Sala delle Prospettive; the Villa Farnesina is set amid tranquil gardens; detail of a vibrant ceiling fresco by Peruzzi; Chigi's bedroom has an ornate ceiling and a fresco by Il Sodoma depicting the wedding night of Alexander the Great

In 1580, the villa was bought by the Farnese family, and it has been known as the Villa Farnesina ever since.

Lots to admire On the ground floor are the Loggia of Galatea, with a much-admired fresco by Raphael of the *Triumph of Galatea*, and the Loggia of Cupid and Psyche, frescoed to Raphael's designs by some of his pupils (including the future star of Mannerist painting, Giulio Romano). On the upper floor is the beautiful Sala delle Prospettive, with a fresco by Baldassare Peruzzi of a *trompe l'oeil* colonnade through which can be seen rural landscapes, villages and a town. Finally, visit Chigi's former bedchamber, decorated with an erotic fresco, *The Wedding Night of Alexander the Great and Roxane*, by Il Sodoma.

THE BASICS

www.villafarnesina.it

⊞ E6

✉ Via della Lungara 230

☎ 06 6802 7268

🕐 Mon–Sat 9–1; guided visits 9–1 on the 2nd Sun of the month

🚌 23, 125, 280 to Lungotevere della Farnesina

♿ Moderate

HIGHLIGHTS

- *Lamine d'Oro*, Sala di Pyrgi: a gold tablet
- The villa's Mannerist architectural style, preferred by Michelangelo
- Vase: *Cratere a Volute*
- Finds from Falerii Veteres
- The gruesome frieze displaying the Greek boxer (400BC) eating the brain of his opponent
- Marriage coffer: *Cista Ficoroni*
- Gardens with Nymphaeum and reconstructed Temple of Alatri

The Museo Nazionale Etrusco di Villa Giulia houses the world's greatest collection of Etruscan art and objects. The exhibits are not always perfectly presented, but it is a revelation to discover this mysterious and sophisticated civilization.

The villa Built between 1550 and 1555 as a country house and garden for the hedonistic Pope Julius III, the Villa Giulia was designed by some of the leading architects of the day, including Michelangelo, Giacomo da Vignola and Giorgio Vasari.

The collection The exhibits are generally divided between finds from Etruscan sites in northern Etruria (western central Italy) and from excavations in the south (Nemi and Praeneste),

Clockwise from far left: The ornately decorated semicircular loggia at the rear of the villa; this red-figured skyphos (a wine cup with two handles) forms part of the collection; the sarcophagus depicting a married couple reclining at a banquet in the afterlife is one of the treasures on display

including objects made by the Greeks. Most notable are the Castellani exhibits, which include vases, cups and ewers, and jewellery from the Minoan period (the latter collection is one of the villa's special treasures). To see the most striking works of art, be selective. Pick through the vases noting the Tomba del Guerriero and the Cratere a Volute. Note also the Sarcofago degli Sposi, a sixth-century BC sarcophagus with figures of a married couple reclining on a banqueting couch; the engraved marriage coffer known as the Cista Ficoroni (fourth century BC); the giant terracotta figures, *Hercules and Apollo*; the temple sculptures from Falerii Veteres; and the valuable seventh-century BC relics in gold, silver, bronze and ivory from the Barberini and Bernardini tombs in Praeneste, 39km (24 miles) east of Rome.

THE BASICS

http://villagiulia.beniculturali.it

🔒 G1

✉ Piazzale di Villa Giulia 9

☎ 06 322 6571; online booking, www.tosc.it

🕐 Tue–Sun 8.30am–7.30pm

🍴 Café and shop

🚌 3 or 19 to Viale delle Belle Arti

♿ Good

💶 Moderate

More to See

This section contains other great places to visit if you have more time. Some are in the heart of the city while others are a short journey away, found under Further Afield. This chapter also has fantastic excursions that you should set aside a whole day for.

In the Heart of the City

ARCO DI COSTANTINO

Triumphal arches, like celebratory columns, were usually raised as monuments to military achievement, in this case the victory of Emperor Constantine over his imperial rival Maxentius in AD312. It was one of the last great monuments to be built in ancient Rome, and at 21m (69ft) high and 26m (85ft) wide it is also the largest of the city's arches. Most of its reliefs were taken from earlier buildings, partly out of pragmatism and partly out of a desire to link Constantine's glories with those of the past. The battle scenes of the central arch show Trajan at war with the Dacians; another describes a boar hunt and sacrifice to Apollo.

🞧 J7 ✉ Piazza del Colosseo-Via di San Gregorio, Via dei Fori Imperiali 🕐 Always open 🚇 Colosseo 🚌 60, 75, 85, 87, 117, 175, C3 to Piazza del Colosseo 🎫 Free

AVENTINO

The southernmost of Rome's seven hills is one of the city's most beautiful quarters. Here the traffic and chaos are left far behind, replaced by peaceful churches, charming cloisters, beautiful gardens and panoramic views over Trastevere and St. Peter's.

🞧 G8 🚇 Circo Massimo 🚌 C3, 81, 160, 628, 715 to Via del Circo Massimo

CIRCO MASSIMO

This enormous grassy arena follows the outline of a stadium once capable of seating 300,000 people. Created to satisfy the passionate Roman appetite for chariot racing, and the prototype for almost all subsequent race-courses, it was begun around 326BC and modified frequently before the occasion of its last recorded use under Totila the Ostrogoth in AD549. Much of the original structure was robbed of its stone—old monuments were often ransacked for building materials—but the *spina* (the circuit's dividing wall) remains, marked by a row of cypresses, along with the ruins of the imperial box and the open arena, now a public park. Avoid after dark.

🞧 H8 ✉ Via del Circo Massimo

Cast in evening light, the Arco di Costantino

Always open 🔵 Circo Massimo 🚌 60, 75, 81, 175, 628, 673, C3 to Piazza di Porta Capena ⚫ Free

COLONNA DI MARCO AURELIO

The Column of Marcus Aurelius (AD180–96) celebrates Aurelius's military triumphs over hostile north European tribes. It is composed of 27 separate drums of Carrara marble welded into a seamless whole, and is decorated with a continuous spiral of bas-reliefs commemorating episodes from the victorious campaigns. Aurelius is depicted no fewer than 59 times, though curiously never actually in battle. At the top of the 50m (140ft) structure stands a statue of St. Paul, who replaced the 60th depiction of Aurelius in 1589.

✚ G5 ✉ Piazza Colonna, Via del Corso ⏰ Always open 🔵 Barberini 🚌 62, 63, 85, 95, 117, 119 and all routes to Via del Corso ⚫ Free

CRYPTA BALBI

This museum, part of the Museo Nazionale Romano, contains the ruins of a theatre built in 13BC, along with a collection of objects to illustrate social, economic and urban planning changes from ancient times through the Middle Ages to the present day. Two other sections have displays of vases, glassware, mosaics and other items dating from between the fifth and eighth centuries.

✚ G6 ✉ Via delle Botteghe Oscure 31 ⏰ 06 3996 7700; online booking www.coopculture.it ⏰ Tue–Sun 9–7.45 🔵 Colosseo 🚌 30,40, 46, 62, 64, 70, 492, 628, 780, 787, 916 to Largo di Torre Argentina ⚫ Moderate (combined ticket)

FONTANA DELLE TARTARUGHE

This tiny fountain (1581–84) is one of Rome's most delightful, thanks to the tortoises, probably added by Bernini in 1658 (the current bronze sculptures are copies).

✚ F6 ✉ Piazza Mattei 🚌 H, 8, 63, 630, 780 to Via Arenula or 30, 70, 87, 116 and other services to Largo di Torre Argentina

FONTANA DEL TRITONE

Like its companion piece, the Fontana delle Api, the Fontana

St. Paul atop the Colonna di Marco Aurelio

Fontana del Tritone, Piazza Barberini

del Tritone (1643) was also designed by Bernini for Urban VIII. One of the sculptor's earliest fountains, the Fountain of the Triton depicts four dolphins supporting twin scallop shells bearing the Barberini coat of arms, on which the triumphant Triton is enthroned.
╬ H4 **✉** Piazza Barberini **Ⓜ** Barberini **🚌** 52, 53, 61, 62, 80, 95, 116, 119 to Piazza Barberini or Via del Tritone

FORI IMPERIALI

All five of the Imperial Forums that are featured in the Museo dei Fori Imperiali (▷ 28–29) stretch between the museum area and the Colosseum, and it's worth the walk to see them all. Built as political and commercial hubs by successive emperors, they have been ruthlessly plundered over time, and may seem like a haphazard collection of columns and tumbled stone, but seeing them close-up can be quite momentous. Excavations are ongoing and what has been unearthed represents only half of the original forums.
╬ H6 **✉** Via dei Fori Imperiali **☎** 06 679 7702 or 06 0608 **🕐** Guided tour only, check with museum for times **Ⓜ** Colosseo **🚌** 75, 84, 87, 117, 175 to Via dei Fori Imperiali **🎫** Moderate

GALLERIA DELL'ACCADEMIA DI SAN LUCA

www.accademiasanluca.it
The gallery was founded to promote the training of artists in Renaissance techniques. From 1633, every artist member of the academy had to donate a work of art, resulting in a great collection that includes paintings by Raphael, Canova, Van Dyck, Rubens and Titian, to name a few.
╬ H4 **✉** Piazza dell'Accademia di San Luca 77 **☎** 06 679 8850 **🕐** Mon–Fri 10–12.30 **Ⓜ** Spagna or Barberini **🚌** 52, 53, 60, 61, 62, 71, 80, 85, 160, 850 to Piazza San Silvestro **🎫** Free

GHETTO

www.museoebraico.roma.it
This picturesque place, its narrow streets full of Jewish restaurants, pastry shops and workshops, is still a meeting place for the Roman-Jewish community. The 1904

The ruins of the Temple of Minerva, Fori Imperiali

The early 20th-century synagogue in the Ghetto quarter

synagogue, overlooking the Tiber, houses the Jewish Museum, its dome visible from much of the city.

🕂 F6 Museo: ✉ Lungotevere Cenci ☎ 06 6840 0661 🕐 Mid-Jun to mid-Sep Sun–Thu 10–6.15, Fri 10–3.15 (closes 4.15 rest of year) 🚌 23, 63, 280, 630 💷 Expensive (includes tour of synagogue)

ISOLA TIBERINA

This small island in the Tiber, with its medieval buildings and Roman bridges, feels like a safe haven, protected from the chaos of the city. The island is on a volcanic rock and its shape resembles that of a ship. Two bridges join it to the riverbanks: the Ponte Cestio dates back to the first century BC, and leads to Trastevere; while the Ponte Fabricio, built in 62BC, the only Roman bridge to survive intact, joins the island to the Ghetto.

🕂 F7 🚌 H, 23, 63, 280, 780 to Lungotevere dei Cenci and all services to Via Arenula and Largo di Torre Argentina

MONTE PALATINO

After a stroll around the Forum it's worth making time to climb the Palatine Hill to enjoy this peaceful spot. Orange groves, cypresses and endless drowsy corners, all speckled with flowers and ancient stones, make up the Orti Farnesiani (Farnesian Gardens), which were laid out in the 16th century over the ruins of the palace that once stood here.

🕂 H7 ✉ Entrances from Via di San Gregorio 30 and other entrances to Roman Forum ☎ 06 3996 7700 🕐 Hours as for Colosseo (▷ 19) Ⓜ Colosseo 🚌 75, 84, 87, 117, 175 to Via dei Fori Imperiali 💷 Expensive (joint ticket valid for two days with Colosseo and Foro Romano)

MUSEO DELL'ARA PACIS

www.arapacis.it

Augustus's Altar of Peace, now contained within architect Richard Meier's controversial glass pavilion (opened in 2006) is decorated with bas-reliefs from 9BC. It was built to celebrate Augustus's triumphal return to Rome after campaigns in Spain and Gaul, and to commemorate the peace he had established throughout the Roman world. The outside of the

The Basilica di San Bartolomeo all'Isola, Isola Tiberina

enclosure is decorated with mythological scenes and grand processional friezes in which life-size figures portray Augustus, the imperial family, officials and other notables. Meier's futuristic housing for the altar was the first architectural work built in the historic centre since the fall of Fascism.

F4 ⊠ Lungotevere in Augusta, at the corner of Via Tomacelli ☎ 06 8205 9127 online tickets www.ticketclic.it ⏱ Tue–Sun 9–7 🚇 Spagna 🚌 224, 913 to Piazza Augusto Imperatore or 224, 590, 628, 926 to Lungotevere in Augusta or 117, 119 to Via di Ripetta 💷 Expensive

MUSEO KEATS-SHELLEY

www.keats-shelley-house.org
Since 1909 this house, the final home of Keats and where he died in 1821, has been a museum and library for students of the Romantic poets Keats and Shelley. Books, pictures and essays lie scattered around the 18th-century house.

G4 ⊠ Piazza di Spagna 26 ☎ 06 678 4235 ⏱ Mon–Fri 10–1, 2–6, Sat 11–2, 3–6 🚇 Spagna 🚌 119 to Piazza di Spagna 💷 Moderate

MUSEO NAZIONALE DEL PALAZZO VENEZIA

www.museopalazzovenezia.beniculturali.it
Built in 1455 for Pietro Barbo (later Pope Paul II), and one of the first Renaissance palaces, the former Venetian Embassy became the property of the state in 1916; Mussolini harangued the crowds from the balconies. Visiting exhibitions and a permanent collection including Renaissance paintings, sculpture, armour and silverware.

G6 ⊠ Palazzo Venezia, Via del Plebiscito 118 ☎ 06 6999 4388; reservations 06 328101 ⏱ Tue–Sun 8.30–7.30 🚌 All services to Piazza Venezia 💷 Moderate (expensive during exhibitions)

ORTO BOTANICO

Trastevere has few open spaces, so these university gardens and their 8,000 or so botanical species provide a welcome oasis of green.

D7 ⊠ Largo Cristina di Svezia 24, off Via Corsini ☎ 06 4991 7107 ⏱ Apr to mid-Oct 9.30–6.30 (5.30 mid-Oct to Apr); closed public holidays and Aug 🚌 23, 280 to Lungotevere della Farnesina 💷 Moderate

A 15th-century icon painting, Museo del Palazzo Venezia
View from the Orto Botanico across Rome to Villa Medici

PALAZZO CORSINI

http://galleriacorsini.beniculturali.it

Though in a separate building, this gallery is part of the Palazzo Barberini's Galleria Nazionale. Originally part of the Corsini family's 17th-century collection, it became state property in 1883. Pictures from the 16th to 18th centuries hang alongside bronzes and sculptures in elegant rooms.

➕ E6 ✉ Via della Lungara 10
☎ 06 6880 2323, reservations 06 32810; www.tosc.it 🕐 Tue–Sun 8.30–7.30 🚌 23, 280, 870 to Lungotevere della Farnesina 💶 Moderate

PALAZZO SPADA

http://galleriaspada.beniculturali.it

This pretty palazzo, with a creamy stucco facade (1556–62), has four rooms where you can admire the 17th- and 18th-century Spada family paintings. Cardinal Spada is portrayed by Guido Reni; there's a fine Borromini *Perspective* and works by Albrecht Dürer, Andrea del Sarto and others.

➕ F6 ✉ Piazza Capo di Ferro 13–Vicolo del Polverone 15b ☎ 06 687 4896 or 06

683 2409 🕐 Tue–Sat 8.30–7.30 🚌 H, 8, 63, 630 to Via Arenula 💶 Moderate

PIAZZA DEL CAMPIDOGLIO

This piazza was designed by Michelangelo on the Capitoline, the most famous of Rome's seven hills and the hub of the Roman Empire, for Emperor Charles V's triumphal entry into Rome in 1536. The magnificent buildings that stand on three sides of the square—the Palazzo Senatorio, the Palazzo Nuovo and the Palazzo dei Conservatori—were part of his scheme.

➕ G6 ✉ Piazza del Campidoglio
🚇 Colosseo 🚌 All services to Piazza Venezia

PINCIO

The park was laid out in the early 19th century. Walk to the Pincio from Piazza del Popolo or Piazza di Spagna to enjoy wonderful views (best at dusk) across the rooftops to St. Peter's.

➕ G2 ✉ Piazza del Pincio 🕐 Daily dawn–dusk 🚌 95, 117, 119 to Piazzale Flaminio or Piazza del Popolo 💶 Free

The entrance to Palazzo Corsini

A replica gilded bronze statue of Marcus Aurelius *in the centre of Piazza del Campidoglio*

MORE TO SEE

SAN GIOVANNI IN LATERANO

Until the 14th century, when the Popes moved to the Vatican, San Giovanni was the pontiff's seat and the focus of Christianity. It's no accident that when the fourth-century original was rebuilt in the 17th century after barbarians, earthquakes and fires destroyed it, it was modelled on St. Peter's.

🔡 L8 ⊠ Piazza San Giovanni in Laterano ☎ 06 6988 6493 🕐 Church Apr–Sep daily 7–7; Oct–Mar 7–6/6.30). Cloisters daily 9–6; Oct–Mar 9–5. Baptistery daily 7.30–12.30, 4–6 🚇 San Giovanni 🚌 3, 16, 81, 85 87, 117, 850 to Piazza San Giovanni 🎫 Church free. Cloisters and baptistery inexpensive

SAN LUIGI DEI FRANCESI

The church of the French community in Rome was completed in 1589 and devoted to St. Louis (Louis XI of France). Its Renaissance facade conceals three late masterpieces (1597–1602) by Caravaggio depicting episodes from the life of St. Matthew: his *Calling*, *Martyrdom*, and *Inspiration*.

🔡 F5 ⊠ Piazza di San Luigi dei Francesi 5

☎ 06 688 271 🕐 Fri–Wed 10–12.30, 3–7, Thu 10–12.30 🚌 119 to Piazza della Rotonda or 30, 70, 87, 492 to Corso del Rinascimento 🎫 Free

SAN PIETRO IN VINCOLI

San Pietro in Vincoli is an appealing church with a powerful Michelangelo statue of Moses. Rebuilt in 1475 over a basilica founded in 440, the church takes its name from the chains *(vincoli)* kept in the coffer with bronze doors under the high altar. It is said they are the chains used to bind St. Peter while he was held in the Mamertine prison.

🔡 J6 ⊠ Piazza di San Pietro in Vincoli 4a ☎ 06 9784 4950 🕐 Daily 8–12/12.30, 3.30–7 (Oct–Mar 3–6) 🚇 Colosseo or Cavour 🚌 75, 84 to Via Cavour or 60, 75, 85, 87, 117, 175 to Piazza del Colosseo ♿ Good 🎫 Free

SANT'AGOSTINO

One of the first Renaissance churches in Rome, Sant'Agostino still maintains its Latin Cross plan with apse, chapels and dome. It's worth visiting to see the works of

Statues set in the nave of San Giovani in Laterano

Caravaggio's Inspiration of St. Matthew, *San Luigi dei Francesi*

Caravaggio, Raphael and other fine artists. The first chapel on the left contains Caravaggio's magnificent *Madonna di Loreto*.

✚ F5 ✉ Piazza di Sant'Agostino 🕐 Daily 7.30–12, 4.30–7.30 🚌 116 to Via Zanardelli; 30, 40, 46, 62, 63, 64, 70 to Largo di Torre Argentina; 30, 70, 87, 186 to Corso del Rinascimento

SANTA CECILIA IN TRASTEVERE

Enter the church through a delightful courtyard, with a portico supported by old granite columns and a lily garden with a central fountain. Next you pass a facade designed by Ferdinando Fuga in 1741. Crypt excavations and splendid ninth-century apse mosaics depicting Jesus with saints Paul, Agatha, Peter, Paschal, Valerian and Cecilia are among Santa Cecilia's treasures. Another is the fresco *Last Judgement* (1293) by Pietro Cavallini, the remains of a medieval masterpiece that was mostly lost in an 18th-century restoration of the church.

✚ F8 ✉ Piazza di Santa Cecilia 22 ☎ 06 589 9289 or 06 581 2140 🕐 Mon–Sat 9.30–1, 4–6.30, Sun 11.30–12.30, 4–6.30. Cavallini fresco Mon–Sat 10.15–12.15, Sun 11–12.30. Crypt/excavations Mon–Sat 9.30–12.30, 4–6.30 🚌 23, 44, 125, 280 to Viale di Trastevere or Lungotevere Ripa 🎟 Church free; Cavallini fresco inexpensive; crypt inexpensive

SANTA MARIA IN ARACOELI

Perched atop the Capitoline Hill, Santa Maria in Aracoeli, with its glorious ceiling, fine frescoes and soft chandelier-lit interior, is a calm retreat from the ferocious traffic of Piazza Venezia. The flight of 124 steep steps approaching Santa Maria was built in 1348 to celebrate either the end of a plague epidemic or the Holy Year proclaimed for 1350. The church is first recorded in AD574, but even then it was old. Most of the present structure dates from 1260.

✚ G6 ✉ Piazza d'Aracoeli ☎ 06 6976 3839 🕐 Daily May–Sep 9–6.30; Oct–Apr 9.30–5.30 🚌 40, 44, 46, 62, 64, 70, 80 and all other services to Piazza Venezia ♿ Poor: steep steps to main entrance or ramped steps to Piazza del Campidoglio 🎟 Free

MORE TO SEE

Stefano Maderno's altar sculpture of St. Cecilia in Santa Cecilia in Trastevere (1599–1600)

Fresco of St. Benedict, Santa Maria in Aracoeli

SANTA MARIA DELLA CONCEZIONE

www.cappucciniviaveneto.it

Lying in the crypt of Santa Maria della Concezione, built in 1624, are the remains of 4,000 Capuchin monks, some still dressed in jaunty clothes, the bones of others crafted into macabre chandeliers and bizarre wall decorations. The bodies were originally buried in soil especially imported from Jerusalem. When this ran out they were left uncovered, a practice that continued until 1870.

H4 Via Vittorio Veneto 27 06 8880 3695 Church daily 7–12, 3–7. Crypt (Cimitero dei Cappuccini) daily 9–7 52, 53, 80, 95, 116, 119 to Via Vittorio Veneto Moderate

SANTA MARIA IN COSMEDIN

This lovely old medieval church is best known for the Bocca della Verità (Mouth of Truth), a weather-beaten stone face (of the sea god Oceanus) once used by the ancient Romans as a drain cover. Inside, the church has a beautiful floor, twin pulpits, a bishop's throne and a stone choir screen, all done in fine Cosmati stone inlay. Most date from the 12th century, a little earlier than the impressive *baldacchino* (altar canopy), which was built by Deodato di Cosma in 1294. In a room off the right aisle is a mosaic depicting the *Adoration of the Magi*, almost all that remains of an eighth-century Greek church on the site.

G7 Piazza della Bocca della Verità 18 06 678 7759 Apr–Oct daily 9.30–6; Nov–Mar 9.30–5 30, 44, 81, 95, 170 and other routes to Piazza Bocca della Verità or Lungotevere Pierleoni Free

SANTA SABINA

The lovely basilica of Santa Sabina, on the Aventine Hill, has kept its original fifth-century Early Christian plan almost intact. Next to the church is a beautiful medieval cloister where St. Dominic is said to have planted the first orange tree in Rome, the descendants of which still perfume the monks' garden. At the entrance, behind a front portico, is one of the church's main treasures. The entrance

Bones in the crypt, Santa Maria della Concezione

The Bocca della Verità, Santa Maria in Cosmedin

doors are divided into wooden panels, many of them survivors from the fifth-century church, carved with scenes from the Old and New Testaments.

🔳 G8 ✉ Piazza Pietro d'Illiria 1 ☎ 06 5794 0600 ⏰ Daily 8.15–12.30, 3.30–6 Ⓜ Circo Massimo 🚌 C3, 81, 160, 628, 715 to Via del Circo Massimo 🎟 Free

TEMPIO DI VESTA AND TEMPIO DELLA FORTUNA VIRILIS

The Tempio di Vesta and Tempio della Fortuna Virilis are the two best-preserved ancient temples in Rome—all but one of the 20 columns of the former remain standing. Both date from the second century BC, the first named after its resemblance to a similar temple in the Roman Forum. The origins of the second, and the god Portunus to whom it was dedicated, remain a mystery to this day.

🔳 G7 ✉ Piazza Bocca della Verità 7 🚌 C3, H, 81, 160, 175 and other services to Via del Teatro del Marcello and Piazza Bocca della Verità

VILLA BORGHESE

Rome's largest central park was laid out between 1613 and 1616 as the grounds of the Borghese family's summer villa. This shady retreat has walkways, woods and lakes that are complemented by statues, temples, fountains, a racetrack, playgrounds and the Bioparco, a zoo and ecological centre ideal for those travelling with children.

🔳 H2 ✉ Porta Pinciana–Via Flaminia ☎ Bioparco 06 3614 015, www.bioparco.it ⏰ Daily dawn–dusk; Bioparco daily 9.30–5/6 Ⓜ Flaminio 🚌 3, 19, 88, 95, 116, 117, 119, 495 🎟 Free; Bioparco expensive

VILLA CELIMONTANA

Set on one of the southern hills of ancient Rome and scattered with the remains of ancient buildings, this is one of the city's lesser-known parks, easily accessible from the Colosseum and San Giovanni in Laterano.

🔳 J8 ✉ Piazza della Navicella ⏰ Daily 7–dusk 🚌 3 to Via del Parco del Celio or 117, 673 to Via Claudia 🎟 Free

The Temple of Diana in the leafy park of Villa Borghese

Further Afield

CATACOMBE DI SAN CALLISTO

www.catacombe.roma.it

These second-century catacombs are the largest and most impressive in Rome—and the most popular. They extend over 20km (12 miles) on five levels, with over 170,000 Christian burial places. You can explore claustrophobic tunnels and *loculi*, or burial niches, carved from the soft tufa stone.

✚ Off map at J9 ✉ Via Appia Antica 110/126 ☎ 06 5130 1580 or 06 513 0151 🕐 Thu–Tue 9–12, 2–5; closed Feb 🚌 714 to Piazza di San Giovanni in Laterano, then bus 218 to Fosse Ardeatine 💲 Expensive

CATACOMBE DI SAN SEBASTIANO

www.catacombe.org

Above the catacombs is the fourth-century basilica, dedicated to St. Sebastian, martyred by arrows, where the saint was buried in the third century. The catacombs themselves were some of the most important burial places in early Christian Rome, and may even have housed the bodies of saints Peter and Paul.

✚ Off map at K9 ✉ Via Appia Antica 136 ☎ 06 785 0350 🕐 Mon–Sat 10–5, 2–5; closed 22 Nov–26 Dec 🚌 118, 628 to Via delle Terme di Caracalla 💲 Expensive

MAXXI

www.fondazionemaxxi.it

The Museo Nazionale delle Arti del XXI Secolo, an extraordinary gallery of 21st-century art that opened in 2010, is the work of celebrated architect Zaha Hadid. It includes work from the last 40 years as well as cutting-edge contemporary Italian and international art. It also hosts temporary exhibitions.

✚ Off map F1 ✉ Via Guido Reni 4a ☎ 06 3996 7350 🕐 Tue–Wed, Fri, Sun 11–7, Thu, Sat 11–10pm 🚇 Line A to Flaminio then tram 2 🚌 53, 217, 280, 910 💲 Expensive

MONTE GIANICOLO

www.sanpietroinmontorio.it

It's not one of Rome's original seven hills, but the best view of Rome is from the Janiculum Hill. There are spectacular views all the way up from the Passeggiata del Gianicolo, an avenue that runs

Taking in the panoramic views from the Gianicolo

Zaha Hadid's stunning MAXXI gallery of modern art

around the hill. En route visit the little Tempietto designed by Bramante in 1508, and the church of San Pietro in Montorio.

➕ D7 ✉ Passeggiata del Gianicolo
🕐 Tempietto Via Garibaldi 33 Tue–Sat 9.30–12.30, 2–4.30 (2–4 Nov–Apr); church daily 9–12, 3–6 🚌 44, 75, 115, 125 to the Gianicolo or Via Garibaldi

SAN PAOLO FUORI LE MURA

www.basilicasanpaolo.org

St. Paul outside the Walls marks the spot where St. Paul was buried after his execution in AD67. Begun in AD385, it replaced several smaller churches on the site. It was one of the city's most richly decorated buildings, but a catastrophic fire in 1823 destroyed both the church and most of its treasures. Much of the vast church you see today dates from the 19th century, though one or two artistic masterpieces survived the fire, notably a beautiful altar canopy by Arnolfo di Cambio dating from 1285.

➕ Off map G9 ✉ Piazzale San Paolo 1, Via Ostiense 186 ☎ 06 6988 0800/0801
🕐 Daily 🚇 Line B to Basilica di San Paolo

🚌 23 to Ostiense/LGT San Paolo or 271 to Viale di San Paolo 🎫 Church free

TERME DI CARACALLA

Ancient Rome's luxurious baths could hold as many as 1,600 bathers. Started by Septimius Severus in AD206, and completed 11 years later by his son, Caracalla, they were designed for gatherings as well as for hygiene. The site is now used for outdoor opera.

➕ J9 ✉ Via delle Terme di Caracalla 52 ☎ 06 575 8626 Online tickets www.coopculture.it 🕐 Tue–Sun 9–1 hour before sunset, Mon 9–2; closed public holidays 🚇 Circo Massimo 🚌 60, 75, 81, 175, 673 to Via di San Gregorio-Via delle Terme di Caracalla 🎫 Moderate (combined Appia Antica Card also gives admission to tombs on Via Appia Antica)

VILLA DORIA PAMPHILJ

If you fancy a good long walk away from the crowds, there is nowhere better than this huge area of green space, Rome's largest park.

➕ B8 ✉ Via di San Pancrazio 🕐 Daily dawn–dusk 🚌 44, 75, 870 to the Gianicolo or 115, 125 to Via Garibaldi

San Paolo Fuori le Mura's apse mosaic depicting Christ flanked by the Apostles

Rome's public baths, Terme di Caracalla

Excursions

FRASCATI

Frascati is the loveliest of the Castelli Romani, 13 towns in the Colli Albani, south of Rome, so-called because they grew up around the feudal castles of the city's popes and patrician families. The Colli Albani are 60km (37 miles) of volcanic hills, known for their wine, lakes, pockets of pretty countryside and—above all—as a refuge from the summer heat of Rome.

Many of the Castelli were damaged during fighting in 1944, and modern building has spoiled some of the towns. Frascati, however, retains much of its charm, and is also the easiest town to reach from central Rome. Come by train and you are rewarded with an appealing ride through some of the Roman Campagna (countryside) as the line climbs into the hills.

The chances are that if you drink house white wine in Rome's restaurants it will come from Frascati, or near by, but the locals like to say it is best drunk *sul posto* (on the spot). There are any number of cafés and *fraschette* (taverns) dotted around the pedestrian-only old quarter—one of the most historic is the Grappolo d'Oro at Piazza Fabio Filzi 5; or visit the stalls in Piazza del Mercato.

The grandest of Frascati's villas is the Villa Aldobrandini, above Piazza Marconi. It was designed in 1598 by Giacomo della Porta for Cardinal Aldobrandini, a nephew of Pope Clement VII. The great villa itself, all faded majesty, is rarely open, but visits are generally possible to the wonderful baroque garden. Don't miss the sweeping views from the main front terrace.

Elsewhere, visit the cathedral, the church of Il Gesù, and the town park, formerly the gardens of the Villa Torlonia, which was destroyed in 1944.

Distance: 20km (12 miles)
Journey time: 30–40 min
🚆 Train from Termini 🚌 COTRAL bus from Anagnina metro station

Villa Aldobrandini

✉ Via Cardinale Massaia 112 🕐 Garden only Apr–Nov Mon–Fri 9–1, 3–6; Dec–Mar Mon–Fri 9–1, 3–4 💶 Moderate

Views of the countryside around Frascati
The terraces at Villa Aldobrandini are decorated with statues

TIVOLI

Tivoli is one of the most popular excursions form Rome, thanks to the town's lovely wooded position on a bend of the River Aniene, the superlative gardens of the Villa d'Este and the ruins and grounds of Hadrian's Roman villa. The town can be busy, especially at weekends, and to see everything in a day you will need to arrive early.

The Este gardens were laid out in 1550 as part of a country retreat for Cardinal Ippolito d'Este, son of Lucrezia Borgia and the Duke of Ferrara. Highlights among the gardens' beautiful terraces and fountains are the Fontana dell'Organo (Organ Fountain), which plays tunes, and the Fontana della Civetta (Owl Fountain), which spouts birdsong.

Also worth seeing is the Villa Gregoriana, a more unkempt park created in 1831. Explore the paths through the park's gorge for some fine views of the luxuriant vegetation and two crashing waterfalls.

Hadrian's Villa, the Villa Adriana, requires a trip out of town, but it is well worth it for its romantic complex of Classical ruins. The largest villa discovered in the Roman Empire, it was built between AD118 and AD135 as a retirement home for Emperor Hadrian and covered an area greater than the centre of Imperial Rome.

Distance: 31km (19 miles)
Journey time: 40 min
🚆 Train from Termini 🚌 COTRAL bus from Via Gaeta or metro line B to Ponte Mammolo and then COTRAL bus to Tivoli

Villa d'Este
www.villadestetivoli.info
✉ Piazza Trento ☎ 199 766 166 (call centre) online www.vivaticket.it 🕐 Tue–Sun 8.30–1 hour before dusk; last admission 90 min before closing 💶 Expensive

Villa Gregoriana
✉ Piazza Tempio di Vesta and Largo Sant' Angelo ☎ 0774 3996 7701; www.villagregoriana.it 🕐 Apr to mid-Oct Tue–Sun 10–6.30; Mar, mid-Oct to Nov Tue–Sat 10–4, Sun and public hols 10–4 💶 Moderate

Villa Adriana
www.villaadriana.beniculturali.it
✉ Via di Villa Adriana–Via Tiburtina ☎ 0774 382 733 🕐 Daily 🚌 CAT shuttle bus 4 or 4X from Tivoli centre 💶 Moderate

The Organ Fountain in the grounds of the Villa d'Este

City Tours

This section contains self-guided tours that will help you explore the sights in each of the city's areas. Each tour is designed to take one or two days, with a map pinpointing the recommended places along the way. There is a quick reference guide at the end of each tour, listing everything you need in that area, so you know exactly what's close by.

CITY TOURS

The Ancient City

Ancient monuments can be found across present-day Rome, but the heart of the ancient city centres on an area containing the Roman Forum, the Colosseum and several other majestic ruins, along with magnificent churches and grand museums.

Morning
Start your day in **Piazza Venezia** and admire the **Monumento a Vittorio Emanuele II**, the vast white edifice that dominates this big and busy square. Then climb the ramp, designed by Michelangelo, to **Piazza del Campidoglio** (▷ 71) and pay a quick visit to **Santa Maria in Aracoeli** (▷ 73). Exit the piazza down the lane in its far left corner for a lovely overview of the Roman Forum before descending to Via dei Fori Imperiali to look at the **Fori Imperiali** (▷ 68), located below street level either side of the road. Then allow a good hour or two to explore the **Foro Romano** itself (▷ 22–23).

Mid-morning
The Forum has little shade, so towards the end of your visit climb the slopes of **Monte Palatino** (▷ 69) for a break in its shady gardens. Your Forum ticket is valid for the Palatine and for the **Colosseo** (▷ 18–19), which you should visit next—exit the Forum beyond the Arco di Tito and the amphitheatre is in front of you. Don't overlook the **Arco di Costantino** (▷ 66), on your right just after you exit the Forum, and be sure to join the correct ticket-holders' queue for the Colosseum.

Lunch
Check your watch and, if it's still open, visit **San Pietro in Vincoli** (▷ 72), barely five minutes' walk from the Colosseum. For lunch, avoid the generally poor-quality cafés in Piazza del Colosseo and walk a few minutes to **Cavour 313** (▷ 134) or one of the evening choices (see facing page). Alternatively, eat a picnic in the nearby **Colle Oppio** park.

Afternoon

If you like churches, now is the time to visit **San Giovanni in Laterano** (▷ 72), which is open all day. If you want less of a walk, and a more manageable and fascinating church, restrict yourself to **San Clemente** (▷ 50–51), but note that it does not usually open until mid-afternoon.

Mid-afternoon

Retrace your steps to Piazza del Campidoglio and perhaps take a break on the terrace café of the Monumento a Vittorio Emanuele II, which has good views of the **Fori Imperiali** (▷ 68). If you still have the energy for a museum, see the **Musei Capitolini** (▷ 24–25). If the **Mercati di Traiano** museum (▷ 28–29) sounds more appealing, return to Piazza Venezia, and walk up Via Magnanapoli, with the Foro Traiano on your right, to the museum entrance.

Evening

It is well worth returning here at night, or remaining here at the end of your day, to enjoy the sight of several floodlit monuments, especially the **Colosseo** (▷ 18–19) and **Piazza del Campidoglio** (▷ 71). Climb the steps or take the escalator to the terrace (Largo G. Agnesi) above the Colosseo metro station for an especially good view of the amphitheatre. If it's early and you just want a snack or light meal, try the lunchtime option **Cavour 313** (▷ 134), or the **Oppio Caffè** (▷ 135) in Colle Oppio park; for a fuller meal, the grid of streets east of the Colosseum has several choices, including **Pasqualino** (▷ 149) and **Il Bocconcino** (▷ 143).

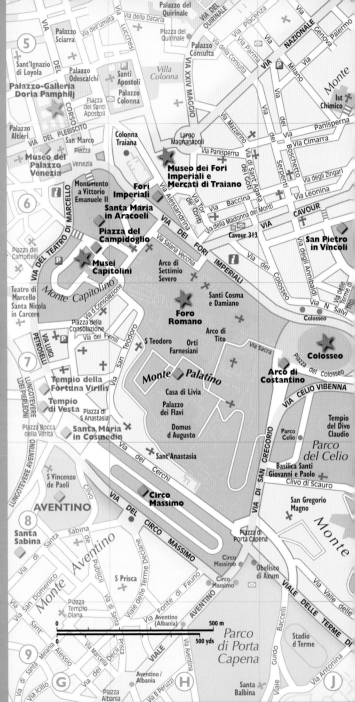

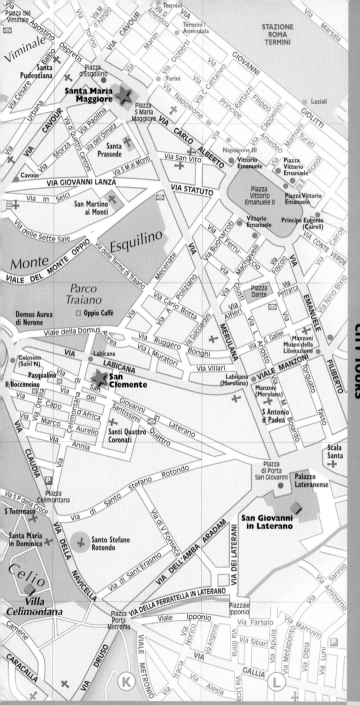

The Ancient City Quick Reference Guide

TOP 25 SIGHTS AND EXPERIENCES

Colosseo (▷ 18)
The Colosseum is the greatest surviving monument from Roman antiquity, a huge amphitheatre built in the first century AD to stage gladiatorial combats and games.

Foro Romano (▷ 22)
Ruins in the Roman Forum span almost 1,500 years, the legacy of an era when this was the political, social, religious and administrative hub of the Roman Empire.

Musei Capitolini (▷ 24)
These two museums on the Capitoline Hill contain Roman and Greek masterpieces, as well as an outstanding collection of Renaissance and other paintings.

Museo dei Fori Imperiali e Mercati di Traiano (▷ 28)
Once the Foro Romano became too cramped, successive emperors created new imperial fora, including Trajan's market complex.

San Clemente (▷ 50)
Three places of worship make up this multi-level complex: a medieval church, an earlier church below and an ancient Roman Mithraic temple below that.

Santa Maria Maggiore (▷ 52)
This fourth-century basilica is one of the great churches of Rome, its vast interior graced with lavishly decorated chapels, and fifth-century mosaics in the nave.

CITY TOURS

Central Rome

Central Rome embraces the medieval, Renaissance and baroque heart of the city, offering a superb variety of palaces, churches, galleries, shops, markets, restaurants and cafés, cobbled streets and fountain-filled piazzas.

CITY TOURS

Morning

Join the market traders early for a cappuccino in **Piazza Campo de' Fiori** (▷ 44–45), being sure to walk into the adjoining **Piazza Farnese** to admire its fountains and the **Palazzo Farnese**. If the small **Palazzo Spada** gallery (▷ 71) appeals, now is the time to see it. Then make your way to the **Pantheon** (▷ 42–43) via Largo di Torre Argentina, Via dei Cestari (known for its shops selling ecclesiastical wear) and **Santa Maria sopra Minerva** (▷ 54–55). From the Pantheon walk to **Piazza Navona** (▷ 46–47) via **San Luigi dei Francesi** (▷ 72), and perhaps pop into **Sant'Agostino** (▷ 72), just north of the square, before it closes around midday.

Mid-morning

Cafés on and around Piazza Navona are often expensive, especially if you sit outside, but it's worth paying over the odds to enjoy the lovely setting. Away from the square, **Caffè della Pace** (▷ 144) is a good bet. So, too, are **La Tazza d'Oro** (▷ 151) and **Sant'Eustachio** (▷ 150) nearer the Pantheon, not so much for their setting but because both claim to offer Rome's best cup of coffee.

Lunch

Before lunch, devote an hour or so to exploring the picturesque streets west of **Piazza Navona**, many of which contain interesting shops and plenty of options for a light lunch. Via del Governo Vecchio, Via dei Coronari and Via dei Banchi Nuovi are especially good, as are Via dei Banchi Vecchi, Via Giulia and Via dei Cappellari west of Piazza Campo de' Fiori.

Afternoon
The afternoon can be devoted to two galleries, with relatively small but superb collections of contrasting exhibits: the Roman sculptures of the **Palazzo Altemps** (▷ 34–35), which is open all day and is a short walk north of Piazza Navona, and the paintings of the **Palazzo-Galleria Doria Pamphilj** (▷ 38–39). Walk between the two via Piazza di Montecitorio and the **Colonna di Marco Aurelio** (▷ 67).

Evening
The area around **Piazza Navona** is one of the city's main restaurant districts, so there are plenty of options (not all good) in the narrow, medieval streets, many of which are lined with tables spilling onto the cobbles on summer evenings. Even if you don't eat or drink here, it's a wonderful, bustling area to walk around. Piazza Navona is a natural meeting place, as is **Piazza della Rotonda** in front of the **Pantheon**. Finish the evening with an ice cream from **Tre Scalini** (▷ 151) or **Gelateria della Palma** (▷ 147).

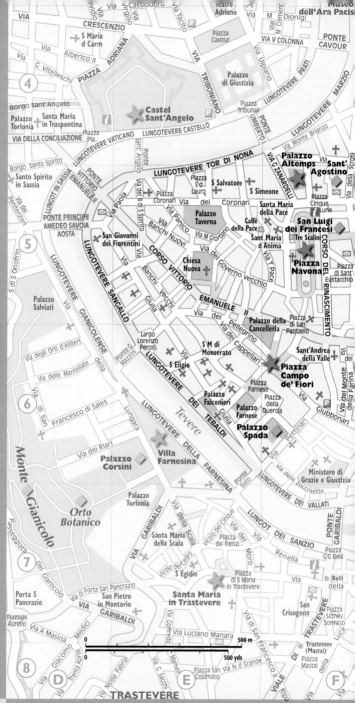

VIA

CRESCENZIO

Via Tacito

Teatro
Adriano

Via

M
Dionigi

M Clement

Museo
dell'Ara Pacis

PONTE
CAVOUR

Piazza
Cavour

VIA V COLONNA

S Maria
d Carm

Via

Alberico II

PIAZZA ADRIANA

VIA TRIBONIANO

VIA G. VITELLESCHI

Palazzo
di Giustizia

LUNGOTEVERE PRATI

LUNGOTEVERE MARZIO

VIA

4

Castel
Sant'Angelo

Piazza
Tribunali

PONTE UMBERTO I

LUNGOTEVERE

Via

Borgo Sant'Angelo

Palazzo
Torlonia

Santa Maria
in Traspontina

VIA DELLA CONCILIAZIONE

Piazza
Pia

LUNGOTEVERE CASTELLO

Via

Monte Brianzo

Borgo santo spirito

Santo Spirito
in Sassia

VIA

IN SASSIA

LUNGOT

EMANUELE II

VITTORIO

PONTE PRINCIPE
AMEDEO SAVOIA
AOSTA

Via dei
Penitenzieri

Via Paola

Via del B di S Spirito

Ponte
Sant'Angelo

San Giovanni
dei Fiorentini

Via Panico

Banchi Nuovi

VIA DELLA VATICANO

LUNGOTEVERE TOR DI NONA

Piazza
S d
Lauro

S Salvatore

S Simeone

Via dei Coronari

Palazzo
Taverna

Santa Maria
della Pace

Caffè
della Pace

Sant Maria
d Anima

Palazzo
Altemps

Via C ZANARDELLI

Sant'
Agostino

Piazza
Cinque
Lune

San Luigi
dei Francesi

Tre Scalini

Piazza
Coronari

Via dei Coronari

Via M Giordano

Chiesa
Nuova

Via del Governo vecchio

Via d Pace

Piazza
Navona

CORSO DEL RINASCIMENTO

Piazza
di Sant
Eustachio

della Scrofa

Via della

5

Palazzo
Salviati

CORSO VITTORIO

EMANUELE II

Banchi
vecchi

Giulia

Via del
Pellegrino

Via dei Cappellari

Via del

Palazzo della
Cancelleria

Piazza
di San
Pantaleo

Sant'Andrea
della Valle

Via del Monte della Farina

LUNGOTEVERE SANGALLO

GIANICOLENSE

Via degli Orti d'Alibert

Via delle Martellate

Ponte G.
Mazzini

Largo
Lorenzo
Perosi

S Eligio

S M di
Monserato

Piazza
Campo
de' Fiori

Giubbonari

6

Via di San
Francesco di Sales

della

Via dei Riari

LUNGOTEVERE DEI TEBALDI

Tevere

S M di
Monserato

Piazza
Farnese

Palazzo
Falconieri

Giulia

Palazzo
Farnese

Piazza
della
Quercia

Palazzo
Spada

Pertinari

via delle zoccolette

Ministero di
Grazie e Giustizia

Lungara

Palazzo
Corsini

Villa
Farnesina

LUNGOTEVERE DELLA FARNESINA

Ponte
Sisto

LUNGOTEVERE DEI VALLATI

PONTE GARIBALDI

Monte Gianicolo

Passeggiata del Gianicolo

Palazzo
Torlonia

Orto
Botanico

VIA GARIBALDI

Santa Maria
della Scala

Via della

Via del Cedro

Vicolo del Cedro

Via dei Cinque

Piazza
de' Renzi

Via del
Moro

LUNGOT DEI SANZIO

Renella

Piazza
G G Belli

Belli

della

7

Porta S
Pancrazio

VIA DI PORTA SAN PANCRAZIO

San Pietro
in Montorio

Santa Maria
in Trastevere

S Egidio

Piazza
di S Maria
in Trastevere

San
Crisogono

Via

TRASTEVERE

Piazza
Sidney
Sonnino

Luce

Piazzale
Aurelio

Medici

VIA GARIBALDI

Via Coffredo

Via Luciano Manara

Via di S Francesco a Ripa

Ripa

DI

8

Giacomo

Via A Masina

Via Trenta Aprile

Via G Sacchi

Via N d Grande

Piazza San
Cosimato

Piazza
Mastai

Via della

0   500 m
0   500 yds

D   E   F

TRASTEVERE

Mausoleo di Augusto

VIA DELLE CARROZZE

Piazza di Spagna

Museo Keats-Shelley

Santa Maria della Concezione

SS Ambrogio e Carlo al Corso

Via Tomacelli

Palazzo Borghese

Via dell' Arancio

Via Font Borghese

Palazzo Ruspoli

Via del Leone

San Lorenzo in Lucina

Via della Mercede

Fontana del Tritone

Piazza Barberini

Barberini Fontana Trevi

Galleria dell' Accademia di San Luca

Via del Prefetti

Palazzo di Montecitorio

Palazzo Chigi

Colonna di Marco Aurelio

Fontana di Trevi

Museo Nazionale delle Paste Alimentari

La Maddalena

Gelateria della Palma

Piazza Montecitorio

Piazza Colonna

Via delle Muratte

Palazzo del Quirinale

Monte Quirinale

Sant'Ivo alla Sapienza

Via Pastini

La Tazza d'Oro

Via del Seminario

Pantheon

Sant'Ignazio di Loyola

Palazzo Sciarra

Piazza del Quirinale

Palazzo Consulta

VIA XXIV MAGGIO

Sant' Eustachio

Piazza della Minerva

Santa Maria sopra Minerva

Palazzo-Galleria Doria Pamphilj

Palazzo Odescalchi

Santi Apostoli

Palazzo Colonna

Villa Colonna

VIA NAZIONALE

Via di Torre Argentina

Palazzo Altieri

VIA DEL PLEBISCITO

San Marco

Piazza del Santi Apostoli

Colonna Traiana

Largo Magnanapoli

Sudario

CORSO VITTORIO EMANUELE II

Chiesa del Gesù

Museo del Palazzo Venezia

Piazza Venezia

Via Panisperna

Museo dei Fori Imperiali e Mercati di Traiano

Argentina

Templi Repubblicani

Via delle Botteghe Oscure

Monumento a Vittorio Emanuele II

Fori Imperiali

Santa Maria in Aracoeli

Via Baccina

Crypta Balbi

Piazza del Campidoglio

VIA DEI FORI IMPERIALI

VIA CAVOUR

GHETTO

Fontana delle Tartarughe

Piazza Campitelli

Musei Capitolini

Arco di Settimio Severo

Santi Cosma e Damiano

LUNGOTEVERE DEI CENCI

Teatro di Marcello

Piazza Monte Savello

Monte Capitolino

Foro Romano

Arco di Tito

Isola Tiberina

Santa Nicola in Carcere

Piazza della Consolazione

S Teodoro

Orti Farnesiani

LUNGOT DELL' ANGUILLARA

San Bartolomeo all' Isola

Monte Palatino

Lungaretta

PONTE PALATINO

Tempio della Fortuna Virilis

Casa di Livia

Palazzo dei Flavi

Via dei Genovesi

Tempio di Vesta

Piazza di S.Anastasia

Domus d'Augusto

Piazza Bocca della Verità

Santa Maria in Cosmedin

Sant'Anastasia

Santa Cecilia in Trastevere

VIA DEL CIRCO MASSIMO

G

AVENTINO

Circo Massimo

H

Central Rome Quick Reference Guide

TOP 25 SIGHTS AND EXPERIENCES

Palazzo Altemps (▷ 34)
This exquisite Renaissance palace
plays host to some of the greatest
of all Roman sculptures, among
them Aphrodite's throne.

**Palazzo-Galleria Doria
Pamphilj (▷ 38)**
This vast palace has over 1,000
rooms and is home to a priceless
collection of Italian art.

Pantheon (▷ 42)
Emperor Hadrian's temple is the
world's best-preserved Roman
monument, with an awe-inspiring
entrance and a beautiful interior.

Piazza Campo de' Fiori (▷ 44)
The 'Field of Flowers' is ringed with
cafés and bars and holds a lively
and colourful traditional food and
flower market.

Piazza Navona (▷ 46)
Rome's most elegant piazza
contains a church and fountains
designed by baroque architects
Bernini and Borromini.

**Santa Maria sopra Minerva
(▷ 54)**
Discover a statue by Michelangelo
and a sublime Renaissance fresco
cycle in this lovely Gothic church.

MORE TO SEE	**64**

Colonna di Marco Aurelio
Crypta Balbi
Fontana delle Tartarughe
Museo del Palazzo Venezia

Palazzo Spada
San Luigi dei Francesi
Sant'Agostino

CITY TOURS

Trastevere and the South

The former Ghetto and picturesque Trastevere area are off the beaten track and more traditional quarters, full of narrow streets, local markets and neighbourhood bars and restaurants.

Morning
Start in **Piazza Mattei**, a little square at the heart of the small grid of streets that was once Rome's Jewish **Ghetto** (▷ 68). It is easily reached from Piazza Venezia to the east, Via Arenula to the west or Via delle Botteghe Oscure to the north. The piazza is home to the charming **Fontana delle Tartarughe** (▷ 67). Take Via della Reginella south out of the square and turn left down Via Portico d'Ottavia to the **Portico d'Ottavia**, the ruined Roman gateway that gives the street its name. It was built as part of a massive complex by Emperor Augustus in the first century BC and dedicated to his sister, Octavia. Today it forms part of the church of **Sant'Angelo in Pescheria**, to its left, which takes its name from the fish market *(forum piscarium)* that flourished on the site from Roman times until the Middle Ages.

Mid-morning
Explore the pretty labyrinth of little streets north of the Portico, then return to Via Portico d'Ottavia and follow it left and south past the Teatro di Marcello to the river and the synagogue and its **museum** (▷ 68). Cross the Ponte Fabricio in front of you and walk around the **Isola Tiberina** (▷ 69), with a visit (if open) to the church of **San Bartolomeo**. Cross the Ponte Cestio to the Trastevere area. Not far from the bridge is the church of **Santa Cecilia in Trastevere** (▷ 73).

Lunch
The most attractive part of Trastevere, and the area with the best choice of places for lunch, lies on the west side of Viale di Trastevere. You may want to eat here this evening, so consider a café snack or buy a picnic, perhaps from the stalls of the market in Piazza di San Cosimato.

Afternoon

Sometimes **Santa Maria in Trastevere** (▷ 58–59) is open all day; sometimes it closes for a period between around 1 and 3. If it is still shut when you have finished lunch, explore some of the streets near by, then see the church. Afterwards, walk down Via della Scala and Via della Lungara to see the **Villa Farnesina** (▷ 60–61). If time allows, see nearby **Palazzo Corsini** (▷ 71) and/or take a break in the **Orto Botanico** (▷ 70).

Evening

Trastevere comes alive in the evenings, especially on and around Piazza di Santa Maria in Trastevere. Admire the floodlit mosaics on the facade of Santa Maria di Trastevere; enjoy the street life in the small lanes near by; and perhaps take a drink in the earthy **Bar San Calisto** (▷ 133).

Dinner

Trastevere has several traditional restaurants, such as the inexpensive **Augusto** (▷ 143) or more refined **Paris** (▷ 149), as well as many pizzerias, of which **Ivo** (▷ 148) and **Dar Poeta** (▷ 146) are classic examples. But it also has a new breed of contemporary dining options, such as **Glass Hosteria** (▷ 147), many of which are gathered around Piazza Trilussa.

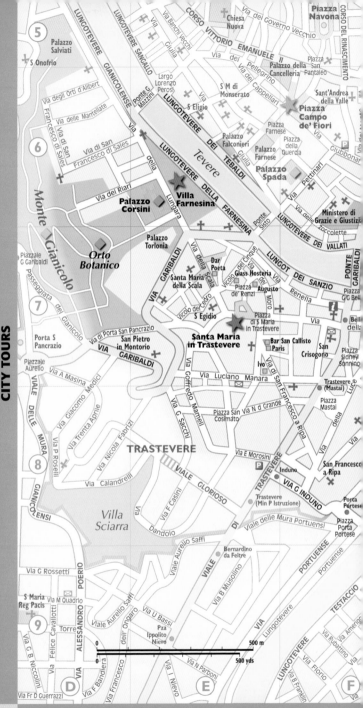

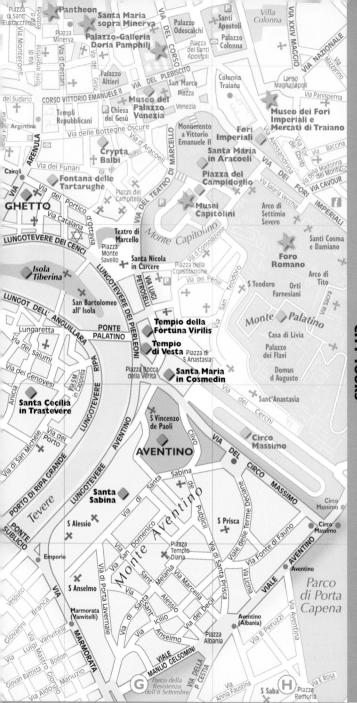

Trastevere and the South
Quick Reference Guide

Santa Maria in Trastevere (▷ 58)

In a neighbourhood of narrow streets, the 12th- to 13th-century church, with a Romanesque bell-tower and mosaic-filled facade, and its square (Piazza Santa Maria in Trastevere) stand out. Both are especially lovely at night, when they are floodlit. The interior of the church is lined with Roman columns and baroque chapels under a sumptuous painted ceiling and a series of glittering mosaics.

Villa Farnesina (▷ 60)

Trastevere, for the most part, has historically been a poorer area of the city. Most of Rome's great palaces were built elsewhere. The Villa Farnesina is an exception, originally created for a Tuscan banker and later bought by the powerful Farnese family. More intimate than its neighbours across the river, it is best known for its lovely interior decoration, and for the frescoes designed and painted by Raphael and Baldassare Peruzzi.

MORE TO SEE	**64**

Aventino
Ghetto
Isola Tiberina
Orto Botanico
Palazzo Corsini
Santa Cecilia in Trastevere
Santa Maria in Cosmedin
Santa Sabina
Tempio di Vesta and Tempio di Fortuna Virilis

CITY TOURS

Northern Rome

Northern Rome embraces historic and more recent areas of the city, as well landmark sights such as Piazza di Spagna and the Fontana di Trevi, along with central Rome's principal park and several of its major galleries.

Morning
Most of Northern Rome's sights are too far away and too widely separated to see in a single, coherent itinerary. Four are also major galleries, two of which are probably enough for one day. If the Etruscans appeal, take a taxi to and from the **Villa Giulia** (▷ 62–63) and make this a self-contained visit. The same goes for the **Museo e Galleria Borghese** (▷ 30–31), though here you could walk back towards the city centre through the **Villa Borghese** (▷ 75) and via the **Pincio gardens** (▷ 71) to Piazza del Popolo (to see **Santa Maria del Popolo**, ▷ 56–57) and from there along to **Piazza di Spagna** (▷ 48–49) on Via Margutta or Via del Babuino.

Mid-morning
Alternatively, you could walk from the Museo directly to **Piazza di Spagna** (▷ 48–49), descending the Spanish Steps, where you'll find the **Museo Keats-Shelley** (▷ 70). This is another museum, but a small one, and its displays—devoted to the English Romantic poets and their circle—are in marked contrast to other galleries and museums of Roman, medieval or Renaissance art and sculpture in the area. If the museum does not appeal, take a break in one of the cafés on or near Piazza di Spagna or explore the many chic shops in the grid of streets around Via Condotti.

Lunch
Restaurants around Piazza di Spagna and Via Condotti tend to be expensive. You'll find better value and more choice west of **Via del Corso**, a slightly less exclusive shopping street. Better still, walk up Via Margutta or Via del Babuino (or a longer route via the Pincio) to **Piazza del Popolo**, which has several cafés for a snack lunch. Or, for a treat, eat at **Le Jardin de Russie** (▷ 148) in the Le Russie hotel, but note that this will not be cheap.

CITY TOURS

Afternoon

If you have lunched near Piazza del Popolo, then you'll be well-placed to see the controversial **Museo dell'Ara Pacis** (▷ 69). This will leave you slightly out on a limb, however, and you might prefer to make straight for the **Fontana di Trevi** (▷ 20–21), but be prepared for the crowds that throng the fountain day and night. You are now reasonably close to the spooky **Santa Maria della Concezione** (▷ 74) and **Palazzo Barberini** (▷ 36–37), but if you have already seen the Mueso e Galleria Borghese, note that the art here is from a similar period.

Mid-afternoon

Instead, consider the Roman collection of the **Palazzo Massimo alle Terme** (▷ 40–41), but take a bus or a taxi from Via del Tritone, as the walk—unless you wend through the back streets between Via del Quirinale and Via Nazionale—is unappealing. The museum is close to Termini station for buses or taxis back to your hotel.

Evening

If you haven't been there for lunch, it is well worth treating yourself to an early evening drink at **Le Jardin de Russie** (▷ 148), especially on a summer's evening. A few minutes' walk would then take you to **Matricianella** (▷ 148) for dinner, a restaurant that is well placed for a stroll after eating to admire a floodlit Fontana di Trevi or to buy an ice cream at **Il Gelato di San Crispino** (▷ 147), not far from the famous fountain.

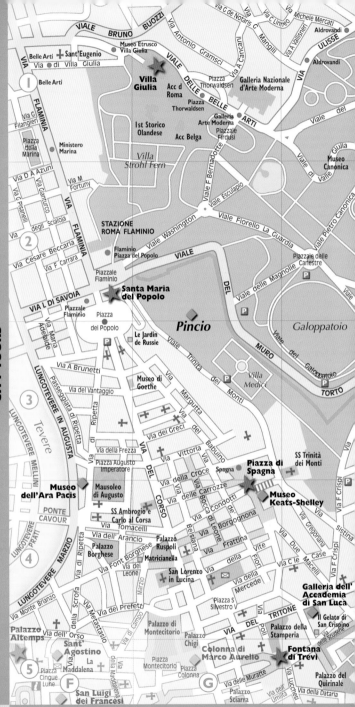

CITY TOURS

Villa Giulia

Museo Etrusco
Villa Giulia

Belle Arti ✝ Sant'Eugenio
Via di Villa Giulia

Belle Arti

VIALE BRUNO BUOZZI

Via Antonio Gramsci

VIALE DELLE BELLE ARTI

Via A Cancani

Via G Filangieri

FLAMINIA

Piazza della Marina

Ministero Marina

Acc d Roma

Piazza Thorwaldsen

Piazza Thorwaldsen

Galleria Arte Moderna

Acc Belga

1st Storico Olandese

Galleria Nazionale d'Arte Moderna

Piazzale Firdusi

Via di Valle

Viale del

Museo Canonica

Viale Pietro Canonica

Villa Strohl Fern

Via D A Azuni

Via C Pisanelli

Via degli Scialoja

Via M Fortuny

Via Canturco

VIA FLAMINIA

Via Cesare Beccaria

Via F Carrara

STAZIONE ROMA FLAMINIO

Viale Washington

Viale Esculapio

Viale Fiorello La Guardia

Flaminio Piazza del Popolo

VIALE

DEL

Piazzale delle Canestre

Piazzale Flaminio

Viale delle Magnolie

Santa Maria del Popolo

Pincio

Galoppatoio

VIA L DI SAVOIA

Piazzale Flaminio

Piazza del Popolo

Le Jardin de Russie

Viale Trinità dei Monti

MURO TORTO

Viale del Galoppatoio

Piazza Maria Adelaide

LUNGOTEVERE IN AUGUSTA

Via A Brunetti

Museo di Goethe

Villa Medici

LUNGOTEVERE MELLINI

Tevere

Passeggiata di Ripetta

Via del Vantaggio

Via di Ripetta

Via della Frezza

Via dell' Oca

Via del Greci

Via del Babuino

SS Trinità dei Monti

Via F Crispi

Piazza Augusto Imperatore

Via Vittoria

Via della Croce

Spagna

Piazza di Spagna

Museo dell'Ara Pacis

Mausoleo di Augusto

SS Ambrogio e Carlo al Corso

Via Tomacelli

Via delle Bocca di Leone

Via Condotti

Museo Keats-Shelley

PONTE CAVOUR

LUNGOTEVERE PRATI

LUNGOTEVERE MARZIO

Via di Ripetta

Via dell'Arancio

Palazzo Ruspoli

Belsiana

Via Borgognona

Via Frattina

Via Vite

Via gregoriana

Via Due Case

Via C le Macelli

Palazzo Borghese

Via Font Borghese

Matricianella

Galleria dell' Accademia di San Luca

Via Monte Brianzo

Via della Scrofa

Via Font Borghese

Via del Leone

San Lorenzo in Lucina

Via della Mercede

Via della Fior

Sistina

Via F Crispi

Palazzo Altemps

Via dell' Orso

Sant' Agostino

La Maddalena

Via dei Prefetti

Via di Campo

Palazzo di Montecitorio

Palazzo Chigi

Piazza s Silvestro V

VIA DEL TRITONE

Palazzo della Stamperia

Il Gelato di San Crispino

Piazza Cinque Lune

Via dell' Umiltà

Via della Dataria

Via della Scuderie

Piazza Montecitorio

Colonna di Marco Aurelio

Piazza Colonna

Via delle Muratte

Fontana di Trevi

Palazzo Sciarra

Palazzo del Quirinale

San Luigi dei Francesi

Via del Metastasio

Via della Maddalena

Via dell' Umiltà

Via Lucchesi

102

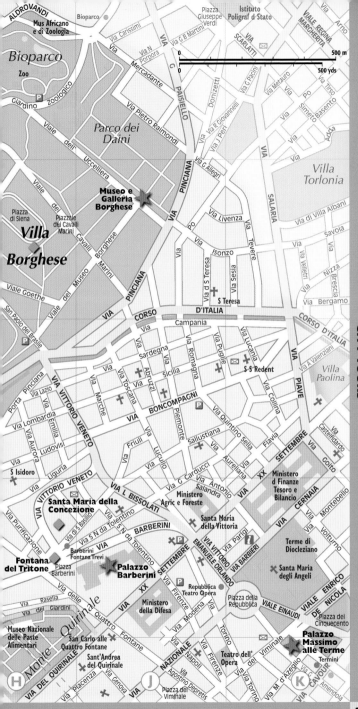

Mus Africano e di Zoologia

Bioparco

Piazza Giuseppe Verdi

Istituto Poligraf d Stato

VIALE REGINA MARGHERITA

Via Carissimi

Via N Porpora

Via G B Martini

Via Arno

Bioparco

Zoo

Giardino Zoologico

Parco dei Daini

Via Mercadante

Via Pietro Raimondi

Via G Allegri

Via R Giovannelli

Via J Peri

Via C Pacini

Via Donizetti

Via Metauro

Villa Torlonia

Via Tirso

Via Po

Via Simeto

Via Basento

Via Adda

PAISIELLO

Via G

PINCIANA

Museo e Galleria Borghese

Piazza di Siena

Piazzale dei Cavalli Marini

Villa Borghese

Viale dell' Uccelliera

Viale del Museo

Borghese

Cavalli Marini

Viale Goethe

San Paolo del Brasile

P

PINCIANA

VIA

Via G Allegri

SALARIA

Via di Villa Albani

Savoia

Via Livenza

Via Tevere

Via Velletri

Nizza

Brescia

Via Po

Via Isonzo

Via S Teresa

Via Sesia

Via Bergamo

S Teresa

CORSO D'ITALIA

Campania

Via Lucania

CORSO D'ITALIA

VIA

PIAVE

Villa Paolina

Via Toscana

Via Sardegna

Via Abruzzi

Via Sicilia

Via Romagna

Via Puglie

S S Redent

Via Collina

Via A Valenziani

VIA VITTORIO VENETO

Via Piancina

Porta Pinciana

Via Lazio

Via Lombardia

Via Emilia

Via Aurora

Via Marche

BONCOMPAGNI

VIA

Via Piemonte

Via Quintino Sella

Via Flavia

SETTEMBRE

Via Castelfidardo

Via Gotto

Via Ludovisi

Via Liguria

S Isidoro

Via Friuli

Via Lucullo

VIA

Via Sallustiana

Via Aureliana

Via G Carducci

XX

Via Antonio Salandra

Ministero d Finanze Tesoro e Bilancio

CERNAIA

Via Montebello

VIA L BISSOLATI

Santa Maria della Concezione

Via di S Basilio

Via S N da Tolentino

Via N da Tolentino

BARBERINI

Ministero Agric e Foreste

Santa Maria della Vittoria

Via Parigi

VIA VITTORIO EMANUELE ORLANDO

VIA BARBIERI

Terme di Diocleziano

Via Volturno

Via Purificazione

Fontana del Tritone

Piazza Barberini

Barberini Fontana Trevi

Palazzo Barberini

VIA

SETTEMBRE

XX

Via Firenze

P

Repubblica Teatro Opera

Piazza della Repubblica

VIALE EINAUDI

Santa Maria degli Angeli

VIALE ENRICO DE NICOLA

Piazza del Cinquecento

Via Rasella

Via del Giardini

Museo Nazionale delle Paste Alimentari

San Carlo alle Quattro Fontane

Sant'Andrea del Quirinale

Monte Quirinale

VIA DEL QUIRINALE

Via delle Quattro Fontane

Ministero della Difesa

Via Modena

NAZIONALE

Via Napoli

Via Agostino Depretis

Piazza del Viminale

Via Firenze

Via Torino

Teatro dell' Opera

Via del Viminale

Via Cavour

Palazzo Massimo alle Terme

Termini

Via Piacenza

Via Genova

Via M d'Azeglio

Via Amendola

H

J

K

CAVOUR

Via Cadorna

CITY TOURS

103

Northern Rome Quick Reference Guide

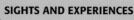

TOP 25 SIGHTS AND EXPERIENCES

Fontana di Trevi (▷ 20)
Throw a coin into Rome's prettiest and most famous fountain and legend says that you will be sure to return to the city.

Museo e Galleria Borghese (▷ 30)
You need to pre-book your visit to enjoy the beauty of the Borghese palace, its paintings and sculptures.

Palazzo Barberini (▷ 36)
Paintings by Caravaggio and Raphael form part of the collection of art and antiquities in this lavishly decorated baroque palace.

Piazza di Spagna (▷ 48)
The Piazza di Spagna is the setting for one of Rome's great sights, the Spanish Steps, and the focus of the city's luxury shopping district.

Palazzo Massimo alle Terme (▷ 40)
A fine setting for some of the city's best Roman and Greek frescoes, murals and sculpture.

Santa Maria del Popolo (▷ 56)
One of Rome's most atmospheric small churches, with sculptures by Jacopo Sansovino and paintings by Pinturicchio and Caravaggio.

Villa Giulia (▷ 62)
Art and artefacts crafted by the Etruscans, the most important of Italy's pre-Roman cultures, form the heart of this large archaeological museum.

CITY TOURS

CITY TOURS

Vatican and Around

Vatican City is an independent state that is home to St. Peter's and the Vatican Museums, a vast complex that contains the Sistine Chapel. Close by is the Castel Sant'Angelo, whose long history has seen it used as a mausoleum, fortress, prison and museum.

Morning

Queues for the **Musei Vaticani** (▷ 26–27) can be extremely long, whatever the time of year, so arrive as early as possible. You will need most of the morning simply to see the highlights of the various museums, but note that you will not be allowed to spend long in the **Cappella Sistina**—such is the weight of people wanting to see Michelangelo's frescoes that visitors are kept moving through the chapel as quickly as the crowd will allow.

Mid-morning

The museums have a café if you wish to take a break from the more than 11km (7 miles) of galleries that make up the complex.

Lunch

Exit the museums and turn right down the hill to Piazza Risorgimento, which has a selection of not terribly good pizzerias and cafés. Better lunch options are available to the north (try **Dal Toscano**, ▷ 146, in Via Germanica) or in the grid of backstreets to the south, an area known as the Borgo: **Borgo Nuovo** (▷ 144) is a particularly good bet. Note that all restaurants in this area are likely to be busy.

Afternoon

It is an easy walk from the Musei Vaticani or the Borgo to Piazza San Pietro and the **Basilica di San Pietro** (▷ 14–15). You will have to queue on the northwest side of the piazza for a security screening before entering the basilica. Queues are shorter later in the afternoon, but note that the church usually closes at 7pm or earlier. This said, you probably won't need to spend more than an hour in the church unless you wish to climb the dome. This leaves time to visit the **Castel Sant' Angelo** (▷ 16–17), an easy walk along Via della Conciliazione. If you didn't want to see the Vatican Museums, a straightforward alternative itinerary might see you visiting the Castel first thing in the morning and the basilica before lunch.

Evening

You should make an effort to linger in—or return to—**Piazza San Pietro** in the evening to enjoy the piazza and the basilica under floodlights. The area does not have as many good dining possibilities as the rest of central Rome, but, if you didn't stop here for lunch, **Borgo Nuovo** (▷ 144), not far from the eastern side of the piazza, is a good choice. For a real treat, take a taxi to **La Pergola** (▷ 149), regarded as one of the city's best restaurants, but dress smartly (jackets for men).

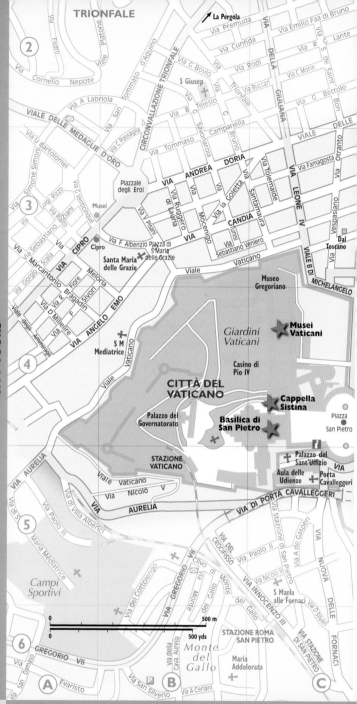

TRIONFALE

→ La Pergola

Piazzale
degli Eroi

Musei

Cipro

Santa Maria
delle Grazie

Piazza di
S Maria
delle Grazie

Museo
Gregoriano

S M
Mediatrice

*Giardini
Vaticani*

**Musei
Vaticani**

Casino di
Pio IV

**CITTÀ DEL
VATICANO**

Palazzo del
Governatorato

**Cappella
Sistina**

**Basilica di
San Pietro**

Piazza
San Pietro

STAZIONE
VATICANO

Palazzo del
Sant'Uffizio

Aula delle
Udienze

Porta
Cavalleggeri

*Campi
Sportivi*

STAZIONE ROMA
SAN PIETRO

S Maria
alle Fornaci

*Monte
del
Gallo*

Maria
Addolorata

0   500 m
0   500 yds

A   B   C

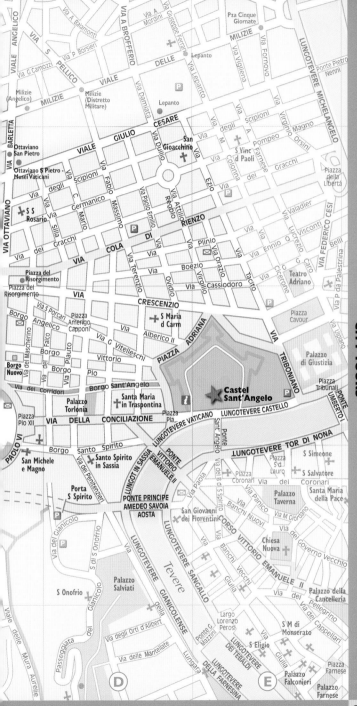

The Vatican and Around
Quick Reference Guide

Basilica di San Pietro (▷ 14)
St. Peter's Basilica was built over the site where the Apostle St. Peter was supposedly buried in the first century. The current church, created over a century, replaced an older church founded around AD326. Piazza San Pietro provides a grand setting for the church, whose vast interior contains a wealth of art and decoration, including Michelangelo's sculptural masterpiece, the *Pietà*.

Castel Sant'Angelo (▷ 16)
The circular bastion of the Castel Sant'Angelo has dominated the banks of the River Tiber since AD130, when the Emperor Hadrian built it as a mausoleum for himself and his imperial successors. In time it became a papal fortress, connected to the Vatican by a covered passageway, and later a prison and a barracks. Today, it is a museum, offering a wide range of papal, military and other exhibits.

Musei Vaticani e Cappella Sistina (▷ 26)
The world's largest museum complex contains many of the artistic treasures accumulated by the papacy in the course of almost 2,000 years. The Sistine Chapel, which lies within the complex, is covered in frescoes by some of the greatest painters of their day, and overarched by Michelangelo's great ceiling fresco and his painting of the *Last Judgement*.

SHOP

EAT

Angel with the Crown of Thorns on Ponte Sant'Angelo

Further Afield

Rome's periphery contains several historical sights, notably a fine bath complex and a cluster of catacombs on the Via Appia Antica. To the east, Tivoli, home to three villas, is one of Rome's most popular excursions. Both of these itineraries can be done as day trips.

DAY 1 Morning
A long morning can easily be devoted to the sights that are gathered conveniently south and southeast of the city centre. Start by taking a bus (118, 218 or Archeobus) or the metro to see the **Circo Massimo** (▷ 66), a large open area that was once a Roman race track, and then the **Terme di Caracalla** (▷ 77), an ancient bath complex.

Mid-morning
Take one of the same buses from the Terme to the cluster of sights concentrated on or near the Via Appia Antica, the well-preserved remains of one of ancient Rome's earliest roads. Here you can see the **catacombs of San Callisto and Sebastiano** (▷ 76), along with the roadside tombs of eminent ancient Romans such as Geta and Cecilia Metella. Not far away are three more catacombs, the **Catacombe Ebraiche** (Jewish Catacombs), **Catacombe di San Domitilla** and **Catacombe di Prestato**.

Lunch
It makes sense to pack a lunch to eat on the **Via Appia Antica**. Alternatively, the area near the start of the Via Appia Antica, around the church of the **Domine Quo Vadis**, has cafés and one or two restaurants, notably **Priscilla** (▷ 150).

Afternoon
Return by Archeobus to Piazza della Bocca della Verità. Cross the river to Lungotevere dell'Anguillara, where you can pick up bus 125 to the corner of Via Garibaldi and Via di Porta di San Pancrazio for a short uphill walk to **Monte Gianicolo** (▷ 76). On your return, either take the same bus 125 or walk back through Trastevere.

DAY 2 Morning

A visit to **Tivoli** (▷ 79) makes the most of a full day, but avoid Mondays, when some sights are shut, and, if possible, weekends, when the town is especially busy with Roman day-trippers. A train from Termini is the best way to get there—take the earliest you can manage and remember to validate your train tickets by punching them in the platform machines. On arrival, make straight for the town's well-signed main villa and garden, the **Villa d'Este** (▷ 79).

Mid-morning

The **Villa d'Este** could easily occupy you all morning, but if you still have an hour or so before lunch, consider seeing the town's second villa, the **Villa Gregoriana** (▷ 79), on the opposite (eastern) side of Tivoli.

Lunch

Tivoli sees many visitors, and offers numerous, often poor-quality cafés and restaurants. **Antico Ristorante Sibilla** (▷ 142–143), which dates from 1730, used to be one such, but the quality of the food and service has recently improved, and the views from the terrace garden over the Aniene gorge are as good as ever. It's convenient for the **Villa Gregoriana** (▷ 79), located on a small street just north of the bridge across the Aniene.

Afternoon

After lunch, return to Piazza Garibaldi, Tivoli's main square, where you can pick up a bus (CAT 4 or 4X) to the third of Tivoli's main attractions, the **Villa Adriana** (▷ 79), whose extensive site should easily keep you occupied for the whole afternoon. Return to Tivoli by bus 4 or 4X and then take the train to Termini (or use bus and metro).

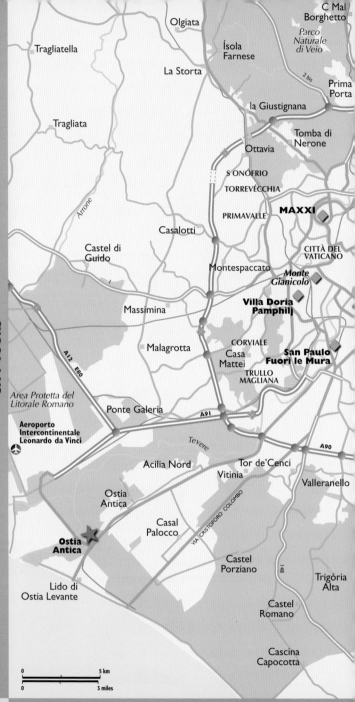

C Mal
Borghetto

*Parco
Naturale
di Veio*

Olgiata

Ísola
Farnese

Tragliatella

La Storta

2 bis

Prima
Porta

la Giustignana

Ottavia

Tomba di
Nerone

Tragliata

S ONÓFRIO

TORREVÉCCHIA

Arrone

PRIMAVALLE

MAXXI

Casalotti

CITTÀ DEL
VATICANO

Castel di
Guido

Montespaccato

*Monte
Gianicolo*

Massimina

**Villa Doria
Pamphilj**

CORVIALE

Malagrotta

Casa
Mattei

**San Paulo
Fuori le Mura**

TRULLO
MAGLIANA

*Area Protetta del
Litorale Romano*

Ponte Galeria

A91

**Aeroporto
Intercontinentale
Leonardo da Vinci**

Tevere

A90

Acilia Nord

Tor de'Cenci

Vitinia

Valleranello

Ostia
Antica

Casal
Palocco

**Ostia
Antica**

Castel
Porziano

Trigória
Alta

Lido di
Ostia Levante

Castel
Romano

Cascina
Capocotta

0   5 km

0   3 miles

Further Afield Quick Reference Guide

Ostia Antica (▷ 32–33)
The present Ostia lies not far from
Fiumicino airport, southwest of
central Rome. Today, it is a small
town and modest seaside resort,
but 2,000 years ago its ancient
Roman counterpart, Ostia Antica—
now some way inland—was the
main port for the imperial city. The
conduit for the immense trade and
riches of empire, it rose to promi-
nence in the fourth century BC,
and remained Rome's port for
around 600 years. As the coast
receded it became landlocked and
was eventually all but covered in
silt and mud. Archaeological
excavations have since revealed
remarkable remains.

MORE TO SEE	64

Catacombe di San Callisto
Catacombe di San Sebastiano
MAXXI
Monte Gianicolo
San Paolo fuori le Mura
Terme di Caracalla
Villa Doria Pamphilj

ENTERTAINMENT	128

Clubs
Alexanderplatz
Piper

Sports
Stadio Olimpico
Six Nations Rugby

EAT	138

Roman/Italian
Antico Ristorante Sibilla
Cacciani
Il Grottino della Sibilla dal 1826

Priscilla
Zarazà

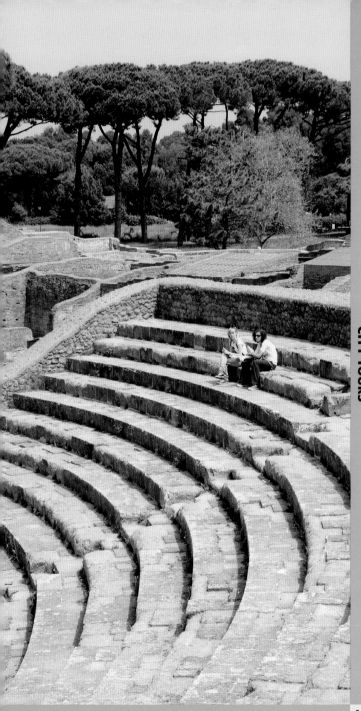

Shop

Whether you're looking for the best local products, a department store or a quirky boutique, you'll find them all in Rome. In this section shops are listed alphabetically.

SHOP

Introduction

Rome was once the market place of an empire that embraced much of the known world. These days it has a more humble place in the shopping firmament. This said, all the great Italian retail staples—food, wine, fashion, shoes, leatherware and clothing—are well represented, and the city is a good source of art, antiques, traditional crafts and artisan products such as furniture.

More for your Money

Mid-price shoes and clothes represent good value for money; you will find them in count-less shops around the new city, but particularly Via Nazionale, Via del Tritone and Via del Corso. The same streets are also dotted with small specialist shops selling good-quality bags, gloves and other leatherware. The sprawling market near Piazza Vittorio Emanuele II, where most Romans do their shopping, is a good source of clothes and shoes, as well as pots, pans and kitchenware with an Italian stamp. In stylish Rome, even inexpensive clothes tend to be good quality and well cut.

Designer Names

At the other sartorial extreme, most of the great Italian and other European fashion houses have shops in the city: Gucci, Prada and Armani are all here, in the grid of streets around Via dei

---

ANTIQUES

It is no wonder, given Rome's long history, that the city is a treasury of antiques. Prices are often high, but the range of objects—Etruscan, Roman, Renaissance, baroque and other items—is unrivalled. For paintings and prints, head for Via Margutta, which also has galleries selling contem-porary art and carpets, while for general antiques try Via Giulia, Via del Babuino (Persian carpets), Via dei Coronari, Via dell'Orso and Via del Monserrato. Also good, and with lower prices and less exclusive stock, are Via del Panico, Via del Pellegrino and Via dei Banchi Nuovi.

Clockwise from the top: Window shopping near Piazza San Lorenzo; an attractive arrangement of bottled liqueurs; hats on a stall in Trastevere; shop in style on

Condotti, an excellent source of high-class clothes, shoes, lingerie and accessories. Department stores have not really caught on, and only Coin and Rinascente are worth a visit.

Tempt your Taste Buds

Shopping for food has a unique charm in Rome, whether in the small area shops known as *alimentari*, or the specialist delicatessens in streets such as Via della Croce. The city's markets, particularly Campo de' Fiori, are vibrant sources of provisions. Pasta, the finest extra virgin oil, *funghi porcini* (dried cep mushrooms), truffle oil and spices make good food buys.

Catholic Paraphernalia

The range of shops selling ecclesiastical items is vast. The largest concentration is around St. Peter's—look out for ceramic Swiss Guards and fluorescent rosaries. On Via dei Cestari all manner of ecclesiastic garb is available—if you ever daydreamed about buying a bishop's robe or a cardinal's hat, this is the place.

Fun for the Visitor

Rome has any number of shops and stalls selling plaster and plastic casts of famous statues. Around the tourist traps are plenty of souvenirs, from figures of gladiators to models of the Colosseum. Better-quality items, plus books, prints and artistic replicas, are sold in museum and gallery shops.

MARBLED PAPER

Notebooks and other stationery items covered with marbled paper make wonderful souvenirs, which you can find in shops all over the city. The paper originated in Venice, where the technique arrived from the East in the 15th century, and is still often handmade. The process involves floating multicolour pigments on liquid gum and combing the different colours into distinctive patterns. The paper is placed delicately on top, then lifted and hung up to dry.

Via dei Condotti, a great place for designer clothes and accessories; cooked meats at a deli on Via Marmorata; religious statues for sale near St. Peter's Basilica

Directory

The Ancient City

Department Stores
Coin
Food and Wine
Bottega del Cioccolato
Panella
Outdoor Markets
Mercato di Via Sannio

Central Rome

Accessories and Leather Goods
Mondello Ottica
Books and Stationery
Cartoleria Pantheon
Feltrinelli
Poggi
Food and Wine
Ai Monasteri
Enoteca Il Goccetto
Interiors
Bassetti
House & Kitchen
Spazio Sette
Outdoor Markets
Campo de' Fiori
Piazza delle Coppelle
Women's Fashion
AVC by Adriana Campanile
Ethic
Fabindia

Trastevere and the South

Books and Stationery
Almost Corner Bookshop
Food and Wine
Drogheria Innocenzi
Volpetti
Interiors
Lumières
Outdoor Markets
Piazza San Cosimato
Porta Portese

Northern Rome

Accessories and Leather Goods
Furla
Gucci
Books and Stationery
Pineider
Department Stores
La Rinascente
Food and Wine
Antica Enoteca
Buccone
Footwear
AVC by Adriana Campanile
Fausto Santini
Ferragamo
Men's Fashion
Battistoni
Ermenegildo Zegna
Women's Fashion
Giorgio Armani
Marella

Vatican and Around

Food and Wine
Castroni
Franchi (Benedetto Franchi)
Religious Artefacts
Streets around St. Peter's

Shopping A-Z

AI MONASTERI

www.emonasteri.it

This unusual, large and rather dark old shop sells the products of seven Italian monasteries, from cosmetics, honeys, wines, natural preserves and liqueurs to herbal cures and elixirs.

➕ F5 ✉ Piazza Cinque Lune 76 (corner of Corso del Rinascimento) ☎ 06 6880 2783 🕐 Fri– Wed 9–1, 4.30–7.30, Thu 9–1; closed part of Aug

ALMOST CORNER BOOKSHOP

This tiny bookshop stocks an interesting and unusual selection of English-language books, especially considering its small size. The prices are competitive, and it is particularly good on biography and history, with a strong emphasis on Rome and Italy. Helpful and knowledgeable staff.

➕ E7 ✉ Via del Moro 45 ☎ 06 583 6942 🕐 Mon–Sat 10–1.30, 3.30–8, Sun 11–1.30, 3.30–8; closed Sun in Aug

ANTICA ENOTECA

www.anticaenoteca.com

An old-fashioned shop where you can buy wine by the bottle or glass, plus snacks and light meals.

➕ G3 ✉ Via della Croce 76b ☎ 06 679 0896 🕐 Daily 11.30am–midnight

AVC BY ADRIANA CAMPANILE

www.avcbyadrianacampanile.com

Bright, modern shoe styles for women with the distinctive red heart logo of Adriana Campanile.

➕ F6 ✉ Largo del Pallaro 1 ☎ 06 6821 0638 🕐 Mon–Sat 10.30–7.30, Sun 11.30–7.30

BASSETTI

www.fratellibassetti.com

A central shop with a dazzling collection of household linen, quality Italian silks and other luxurious fabrics, plus everyday materials.

➕ E5 ✉ Corso Vittorio Emanuele II 73 ☎ 06 689 2326 🕐 Mon–Fri 9–1, 3.30–7.30, Sat 9–1 (hours can vary)

BATTISTONI

www.battistoni.com

A traditional tailor's and shop in business for over half a century. Established in 1946, its clients include many celebrities.

➕ G4 ✉ Via Condotti 60–61a ☎ 06 697 6111 🕐 Tue–Sat 10–7, Mon 3–7

BOTTEGA DEL CIOCCOLATO

www.labottegadelcioccolato.it

A blissful Italian chocolate shop. Most goodies are produced from a 19th-century Piedmont recipe; others are 'secrets of old masters'. There are period cupboards and shelves, and a mirror reflects the chocolate creations along the wall in jars.

➕ J6 ✉ Via Leonina 82 ☎ 06 482 1473 🕐 Mon–Sat 9.30–7.30; closed mid-Jun to Sep

Window shopping

BUCCONE

www.enotecabuccone.com

Close to Piazza del Popolo, this is one of Rome's best-stocked wine bars and wine stores.

➕ F4 ✉ Via di Ripetta 19 ☎ 06 361 2154 🕐 Mon–Thu 9–8.30, Fri–Sat 9am–11.30pm, Sun 11–7

CAMPO DE' FIORI

This picturesque market is in a pretty, central square. Fruit and vegetables dominate, but you can also buy fish, flowers and beans.

➕ F6 ✉ Piazza Campo de' Fiori 🕐 Mon–Sat 7am–1.30pm

CARTOLERIA PANTHEON

www.pantheon-roma.it

Beautiful handcrafted notebooks, exquisite stationery and a wide variety of objects covered in marbled paper are on offer here.

➕ F5 ✉ Via della Rotonda 15 ☎ 06 687 5313 🕐 Mon–Sat 10.30–7.30, Sun 1–7.30

CASTRONI

www.castroni.com

Castroni boasts Rome's largest selection of imported delicacies, a mouthwatering array of Italian specialities and an amazing range of coffees.

➕ D3 ✉ Via Cola di Rienzo 196–198, corner of Via Terenzio ☎ 06 687 4383 🕐 Mon–Sat 8–8

COIN

www.coin.it

One of Rome's most popular department stores, Coin is a modern, mainly glass building with cosmetics, home furnishings, kitchenware, toys and fashions. The top floor is dedicated to home exhibitions. Prices are generally higher than in the average store.

➕ M8 ✉ Piazzale Appio 7 ☎ 06 708 0020 🕐 Mon–Sat 10–8.30, Sun 10.30–8.30

DROGHERIA INNOCENZI

Set on bustling Piazza San Cosimato, this foodie's haven is stacked high with sacks of pasta and polenta, regional specialities and products from abroad that are difficult to find elsewhere. Such is the fame of this shop, people travel from far and wide to stock up, aided by the friendly and attentive staff.

➕ E8 ✉ Piazza San Cosimato, corner of Via Natale del Grande 31 ☎ 06 581 2725 🕐 Daily 8.30–1.30, 4.30–8; closed Th and part of Aug

ENOTECA AL GOCCETTO

www.ilgoccetto.com

Wines from all over Italy are sold in this old bishop's palazzo, complete with original floors and wooden ceiling. Light meals are also served.

➕ E5 ✉ Via dei Banchi Vecchi 14 ☎ 06 686 4268 🕐 Mon 6–12, Tue–Sat 11.30–2.30, 6–12; closed 3 weeks in Aug

---

GIFTS WITH A TWIST

For a souvenir with a difference, visit the extraordinary shops on Via dei Cestari, just south of the Pantheon, which specialize in all sorts of religious clothes, candles and vestments. Crucifixes, rosaries, statues of saints and other religious souvenirs can be found in shops on Via di Porta Angelica near the Vatican. Alternatively, visit the Farmacia Santa Maria della Scala (✉ Piazza Santa Maria della Scala 23, ☎ 06 580 6217, 🕐 Mon–Sat 8.30–1, 4–7.30), an 18th-century monastic pharmacy that sells a variety of herbal remedies.

ERMENEGILDO ZEGNA

www.zegna.com

This is the place to go for informal suits and jackets in exquisite, expensive fabrics. You'll also find stylish shirts, sweaters and a range of accessories.

➕ G4 ✉ Via dei Condotti 58 ☎ 06 6994 0678 🕐 Mon–Sat 10–7.30

ETHIC

An individual Italian chain store with good mid-range fashion just east of Campo de' Fiori.

➕ F6 ✉ Piazza Benedetto Cairoli 11–12 ☎ 06 6830 1063 🕐 Tue–Sat 10–8, Sun–Mon 12–8; closed Sun in Aug

FABINDIA

www.fabindia.it

Facing the Ponte Sant'Angelo is this delightful emporium selling Indian fabrics, scarves and garments, all hand-woven and made in Indian villages. The company is devoted to developing fair and equitable relationships with the producers. The styles are both traditional and more contemporary.

➕ E5 ✉ Via del Banco di Santo Spirito 40 ☎ 06 6889 1230 🕐 Mon–Sat 10–1.30, 3–7.30

FAUSTO SANTINI

www.faustosantini.com

An iconoclast who designs witty, innovative and bizarre shoes.

➕ G4 ✉ Via Frattina 120–1 ☎ 06 678 4114 🕐 Mon–Sat 10–7.30, Sun 12–7.30

FELTRINELLI

www.lafeltrinelli.it

An Italy-wide bookshop chain with shelves displaying a broad range of Italian titles, and usually a reasonable choice of French-, German- and English-language books.

SALES AND BARGAINS

Sales *(soldi)* in Rome are not always the bargains they seem. That said, many shoe shops and top designers cut their prices drastically during summer and winter sales (mid-Jul to mid-Sep and Jan to mid-Mar). Other lures to get you into a shop, notably the offer of *sconti* (discounts) and *vendite promozionali* (promotional offers), rarely save you any money. It can occasionally be worth asking for a discount *(uno sconto)*, particularly if you are paying cash for an expensive item, or buying several items from one shop.

➕ F6 ✉ Largo di Torre Argentina 11 ☎ 06 6866 3001 🕐 Mon–Fri 9–9, Sat 9am–10pm, Sun 10–9

➕ G5 ✉ Galleria Alberto Soldi, Piazza Colonna ☎ 06 6975 5001 🕐 Mon 2–7.30, Tue–Sat 10–7.30

➕ J4 ✉ Via Vittorio Emanuele II Orlando 84–86 ☎ 06 474 6254 🕐 Tue–Sat 9–8, Sun 3.30–7.30, Mon 3.30–8

FERRAGAMO

www.ferragamo.com

This established family firm is probably Italy's most renowned shoe shop. Also sells handbags, small leather goods, men's and women's clothes and accessories.

➕ G4 ✉ Via Condotti 73–74 (women's) ☎ 06 679 1565; ✉ Via Condotti 65 (men's) ☎ 06 678 1130 🕐 Mon–Sat 10–7.30, Sun 11–7

FRANCHI (BENEDETTO FRANCHI)

www.franchi.it

This is quite simply one of the best delicatessens in town, with everything on offer from salamis, cheeses and wines to succulent roast meats and sumptuous delicacies for a picnic.

D3 ✉ Via Cola di Rienzo 200/204
☎ 06 687 4651 ⏰ Mon–Sat 8am–9pm

FURLA
www.furla.com
Offers chic bags, shoes, scarves
and jewellery at more affordable
prices than other designer names.
G3 ✉ Piazza di Spagna 22 ☎ 06 6920
0363 ⏰ Mon–Sat 10–8, Sun 10.30–8

GIORGIO ARMANI
www.armani.com
Armani is the king of cut and
classic, understated elegance.
G4 ✉ Via Condotti 77 ☎ 06 699 1460
⏰ Mon–Sat 10–7, Sun 10–2, 3–7; closed
Sun in Aug

GUCCI
www.gucci.com
Expensive, quality bags, shoes,
accessories and leather goods by
this famous name are for sale.
G3 ✉ Via Condotti 8 ☎ 06 679 0405
⏰ Mon–Sat 10–7, Sun 11–7

HOUSE & KITCHEN
More traditional than Spazio Sette
(▷ below), this shop sells household goods, notably kitchenware.
G6 ✉ Via del Plebiscito 103 ☎ 06
6992 0167 ⏰ Mon–Fri 9–6

LUMIÈRES
This is an unassuming shop
crammed with dozens of antique
lamps. If an interesting lamp from
the French art deco or Italian
Liberty periods is what you're after,
this is the place to come.
E7 ✉ Vicolo del Cinque 48 ☎ 06 580
3614 ⏰ Mon–Sat 10–1, 4–8, Sun 4–8

MARELLA
www.marella.com
The showcase shop for the Marella

label offers classic, well-made
designs at reasonable prices.
G4 ✉ Via Frattina 129–31 ☎ 06 6992
3800 ⏰ Tue–Sat 10–7.30, Mon, Sun 11–2,
3–7

MERCATO DI VIA SANNIO
This market in the shadow of San
Giovanni in Laterano is the place
to come for bags, belts, shoes, toys
and inexpensive clothes. Other
stands near by peddle more interesting bric-a-brac.
M8 ✉ Via Sannio ⏰ Mon–Fri
10–1.30, Sat 10–6

MONDELLO OTTICA
www.mondelloottica.it
Eyewear with a difference: This
minimalist boutique has regular
installations by local artists. Prices
may be higher than average, but
the glasses are superlative in quality and sheer chic. Prescription
glasses can be made within a day.
E5 ✉ Via del Pellegrino 98 ☎ 06 686
1955 ⏰ Mon–Sat 9–1, 3.30–7

PANELLA
www.panellaroma.com
For more than a century, Panella
has sold dozens of varieties of
bread and cakes, and it has the
largest selection of homemade
grissini (bread stick) in Rome. The
back rooms are packed with hard-
to-find ingredients.
K6 ✉ Via Merulana 54–55 ☎ 06 487
2435 ⏰ Mon–Sat 8am–midnight, Sun 8–2;
closed Thu pm Oct–Mar

PIAZZA DELLE COPPELLE
This tiny, attractive local food mar-
ket is an oasis among the cars and
tourists. Close to the Pantheon.
F5 ✉ Piazza delle Coppelle
⏰ Mon–Sat 6am–2pm

Roman supermarkets are few and far between and most food is still bought in tiny local shops known as *alimentari*. Every street of every 'village' or district in the city has one or more of these general shops, a source of everything from olive oil and pasta to candles and corn and bunion treatments. They are also good places to buy picnic provisions—many sell bread and wine—and most have a delicatessen counter that will make you a sandwich *(panino)* from the meats and cheeses on display. For something a little more special, or for food gifts to take home, visit Via della Croce, a street renowned for its wonderful delicatessens.

PIAZZA SAN COSIMATO

It is a shame that very few visitors manage to discover what this excellent mid-size general food market in Trastevere has to offer.
🞧 E8 ✉ Piazza San Cosimato
🕓 Mon–Sat 7am–1pm

PINEIDER

www.pineider.com
Here at Rome's most exclusive stationers virtually any design can be printed onto visiting cards.
🞧 H4 ✉ Via della Fontanella Borghese 22
☎ 06 687 8369 🕓 Mon–Sat 10–2, 3–7

POGGI

Vivid pigments, lovely papers and exquisitely soft brushes have been on sale at Poggi's since 1825. The second shop almost opposite sells high-quality paper.
🞧 G5 ✉ Via del Gesù 74–5 ☎ 06 678 4477 🕓 Mon–Sat 9–1, 4–7.30
🞧 G5 ✉ Via Piè di Marmo 40–1 ☎ 06 6830 8014 🕓 Mon–Fri 9–1, 4–7.30, Sat 9–1

PORTA PORTESE

Everything and anything is for sale at this famous flea market, though the few genuine antiques are highly priced. By mid-morning crowds are huge, so come early, and guard your belongings.
🞧 F8 ✉ Via Porta Portese-Via Ippolito Nievo 🕓 Sun 6.30am–2pm

RELIGIOUS ARTEFACTS

For religious art and souvenirs, both serious and light-hearted, you should head to the streets around St. Peter's, notably Borgo Pio, Via del Mascherino and Via di Porta Angelica.

LA RINASCENTE

www.rinascente.it
This chic department store is good for accessories, cosmetics, designer and mid-range fashion.
🞧 K2 ✉ Piazza Fiume ☎ 06 884 1231
🕓 Mon–Sat 9.30–9.30, Sun 10–9

SPAZIO SETTE

www.spaziosette.com
This is one of the few stores in Rome that will make even the most hardened shopper salivate over furnishings for the kitchen, living room and bathroom.
🞧 F6 ✉ Via dei Barbieri 7 ☎ 06 6880 4261 🕓 Tue–Sat 9.30–1, 3.30–7.30, Mon 3.30–7.30; closed part of Aug

VOLPETTI

www.volpetti.com
This Aladdin's cave of delights has been established for more than 100 years and is justly famous for its handmade pasta, whole hams, cheeses, pungent truffles and extra virgin olive oils.
🞧 G9 ✉ Via Marmorata 47 ☎ 06 574 2352 🕓 Mon–Sat 8–2, 5–8.15

SHOP

Entertainment

Once you've done with sightseeing for
the day, you'll find lots of other great
things to do with your time in this chapter,
even if all you want to do is relax with a
drink. In this section establishments are
listed alphabetically.

Introduction

In such a striking city, and one whose climate is so benign, a stroll on a balmy evening might be all the entertainment you need. At the same time, Rome offers world-class classical concerts, recitals in churches, and plenty of jazz, blues and other live music. Films and productions in Italian mean cinema and theatre are less accessible to most visitors, but opera and sport—notably football and rugby's Six Nations—transcend language. So, too, do the pleasures of a late-night drink or dance in one of the city's many bars and clubs.

Locations

City-centre nightlife focuses on the streets around Piazza Navona (▷ 46–47), which are full of bars, clubs and restaurants, and around Campo de' Fiori, though this area is becoming less salubrious (early evening is the best here). Trastevere has long been popular with visitors, but avoid more down-at-heel corners such as Piazza Trilussa later in the evening.

More popular with Romans are the Testaccio area, south of the city centre (you'll need a taxi), home to many clubs, and—further south still—Via Libetta off Via Ostiense. San Lorenzo, east of Termini station, is a student district, and is always lively (especially around Piazza dell'Immacolata).

SUMMER IN THE CITY

Rome's warm summer evenings are conducive to eating and drinking under the stars or strolling to Piazza San Pietro, the Trevi Fountain, Spanish Steps or Colosseum to people-watch and admire the floodlit monuments. The old Ghetto area is charming after dark, and the Pincio, beyond the Spanish Steps, is a great place to watch the sunset. Festivals take place in the city year-round (visit www.060608.it), but early June to the end of September sees one of the biggest, the Estate Romana (www.estateromana.comune.roma.it), with many free events.

BELLA ROMA

Clockwise from the top: Taking an evening stroll around Piazza della Rotonda; St. Peter's at dusk; top-quality performers can be heard at classical music events;

Il Pigneto, even further out (between Via Casilina and Via Prenestina), is a rough, but increasingly trendy spot for bars and clubs.

The Musical World

The Auditorium-Parco della Musica (▷ 133), Rome's much-loved main performance space, is rightly celebrated for its eclectic programme of classical and other music. The city also has a plethora of small musical associations such as the Associazione La Stravaganza (▷ 133) that organize chamber music and other concerts, often in historic settings. Opera in the city—while not as elevated as in Milan or Naples—also benefits from striking settings, notably the city opera house (▷ 137) and the outdoor Terme di Caracalla (▷ 77). Churches host musical events, not least Sant'Anselmo on the Aventine Hill (▷ 66), where the monks chant Gregorian plainsong nightly at 7.15.

The Night is Free

Plenty of Rome's nightlife and entertainment costs nothing. Church recitals are often free, and some clubs charge nothing, or next to nothing, during the week. Taking an *aperitivo* is increasingly popular, and many bars offer extensive free snacks with an early-evening drink. Festivals throughout the year often have free events, especially those organized by the city council, the Comune di Roma.

NEED TO KNOW

Entry to clubs during the week is usually free, but at weekends you'll pay an entrance fee and may have to buy a *tessera* (temporary 'membership'). Note that many dance clubs close for the summer, or move to outdoor venues on the coast at, or near Ostia. For information on nightlife and cultural events, consult hotel concierges, look for fliers, consult *Trovaroma* (a listings magazine free with Thursday's *La Repubblica* newspaper), pick up *Roma Cè* (free in shops and bars) or visit www.060608.it.

---

enjoy a night of live jazz at a club; there are plenty of bars and clubs to choose from in the city centre; early-evening cocktails are a popular start to the night

Directory

The Ancient City

Pubs and Bars
Druid's Den
Café/Clubs
Oppio Caffè

Central Rome

Bars and Clubs
Anima
Associazione la Stravaganza
Bartaruga
Pubs
Trinity College
Wine Bars
Cavour 313
Cul de Sac
Enoteca Piccola
Escopazzo
La Vineria Reggio

Trastevere and the South

Bars and Clubs
Akab-Cave
L'Alibi
Bar San Calisto

Big Mama
Caffè Latino
Frenie Frizioni
Riparte Café
Wine Bars
Enoteca Trastevere
Cinemas and Theatres
Nuovo Sacher
Teatro Vascello

Northern Rome

Bars and Clubs
Stravinsky Bar
Concert Halls and Theatres
Auditorium Parco della Musica
Teatro Olimpico
Opera
Teatro dell'Opera di Roma

Further Afield

Clubs
Alexanderplatz
Piper
Sports
Stadio Olimpico
Six Nations Rugby

Entertainment A-Z

AKAB-CAVE
www.akabcave.com
In the lively Testaccio area, this very popular and long-established club is on two levels with a garden area and varied music policy. Live rock bands and international DJs.
✚ Off map at G9 ✉ Via di Monte Testaccio 68–69 ☎ 06 5725 0585
⏰ Tue–Sat 11pm–4.30am 🚇 Piramide
🚌 23, 44, 170, 280 to Piazza di Porta San Paolo or Via Monte Testaccio 💷 Expensive

ALEXANDERPLATZ
www.alexanderplatz.it
Historic jazz club with live bands.

✚ Off map ✉ Via Ostia 9 ☎ Information 06 3972 1867 (Mon–Sat 9.30–2), reservations 06 3974 2171 ⏰ Sep–Jun daily 8.30pm–1.30am 🚇 Ottaviano 🚌 23, 70, 490, 913, 991, 994, 999 to Largo Trionfale-Viale delle Milizie 🎫 4-month membership (expensive); usually free to tourists (passport required)

L'ALIBI
www.lalibi.it
Primarily a gay disco, but not exclusively, L'Alibi is one of the most reliable (and most established) clubs that have mushroomed in the trendy area of Testaccio.

➕ Off map at G9 ✉ Via di Monte Testaccio 40–44 ☎ 06 574 3448 🕐 Thu–Sun midnight–5am 🚇 Piramide 🚌 23, 44, 170, 280 to Piazza di Porta San Paolo or Via Monte Testaccio 💷 Expensive

ANIMA

At the heart of a small, buzzing nightlife area, Anima is a welcoming bar and club that plays an eclectic assortment of music and attracts a clientele of all ages.

➕ F5 ✉ Via Santa Maria dell'Anima 57 ☎ 06 6889 2806 🕐 Daily 6pm–4am 🚌 30, 70, 87 and other services to Corso del Rinascimento or Corso Vittorio Emanuele II

ASSOCIAZIONE LA STRAVAGANZA

www.lastravaganzamusica.it

This musical association has been hosting recitals in historic venues around the city since 1980. Locations may include the Palazzo Doria Pamphilj, the Chiostro del Bramante in Santa Maria della Pace (near Piazza Navona), Palazzo della Cancelleria (off Campo de' Fiori) and others.

✉ Via Taurasia 9 ☎ 329 009 9476

AUDITORIUM PARCO DELLA MUSICA

www.auditorium.com

This splendid addition to Rome's classical and contemporary music scene has three concert halls in the shape of enormous grey pods set around a vast open-air arena.

➕ Off Map F1 ✉ Viale Pietro de Coubertin 30 ☎ 06 802411 or 06 8024 1281 🚌 From Stazione Termini shuttle bus M or bus/tram to Viale Tiziano 💷 Moderate

BAR SAN CALISTO

Bohemian and vibrant—this is where the locals hang out. The piazza-side tables give a window on the real Trastevere and cheap prices make it a great spot to linger. Chocolate, hot with cream in winter and cooling as a *gelato* in summer, is among Rome's best.

➕ E7 ✉ Piazza di San Calisto 3 ☎ 06 583 5869 🕐 Mon–Sat 6am–2am 🚌 H, 8 to Viale di Trastevere

BARTARUGA

www.bartaruga.it

This wonderfully baroque and kitsch bar at the heart of the

Dancing the night away in one of Rome's lively clubs

Ghetto has sofas, chandeliers and soft lighting, and offers occasional live music and cabaret.

🔢 F6 ✉ Piazza Mattei 9 ☎ 06 689 2299 🕐 Daily 6pm until late 🚌 H, 8, 271 to Via Arenula or services to Largo di Torre Argentina

BIG MAMA

www.bigmama.it

Big Mama, Rome's best blues club, also hosts rock and jazz.

🔢 F8 ✉ Vicolo San Francesco a Ripa 18 ☎ 06 581 2551 🕐 Mid-Sep to Jun Tue–Sat 9pm–1.30am 🚌 H, 8 to Viale di Trastevere 🎫 Membership (moderate)

CAFFÈ LATINO

www.caffelatinoroma.com

Testaccio's oldest club is devoted to eating, drinking, live music and dance sessions. Mostly jazz, but rap, blues and other genres can also be heard here.

🔢 Off map at G9 ✉ Via Monte Testaccio 96 ☎ 06 578 2411 🕐 Sep–Jul Tue–Thu, Sun 10.30pm–2.30am, Fri, Sat 10.30pm–4.30am 🚇 Piramide 🚌 3, 23, 30, 75, 280, 716 to Via Marmorata 🎫 Membership (expensive)

CAVOUR 313

www.cavour313.it

At the Forum end of Via Cavour, this easily missed wine bar has a relaxed, student feel. There are good snacks from the bar and wine by the glass or bottle.

🔢 H6 ✉ Via Cavour 313 ☎ 06 678 5496 🕐 Mon–Sat 12.30–2.45, 7.30–12.30 (also Sun 7.30–12.30 Oct–May) 🚌 75, 84, 117 to Via Cavour or 84, 85, 87, 175 to Via dei Fori Imperiali

CUL DE SAC

www.enotecaculdesac.com

Rome's original informal wine bar, near Piazza Navona, with pine tables and a big marble bar. More than 1,400 wines, plus snacks, light meals and cheese and salami from every region in Italy.

🔢 F5 ✉ Piazza Pasquino 73 ☎ 06 6880 1094 🕐 Daily 12–12 🚌 46, 62, 64 to Corso Vittorio Emanuele II

DRUID'S DEN

www.druidspubrome.com

A friendly and authentic Irish pub that appeals to Romans and expats alike. Also try the Fiddler's Elbow, a

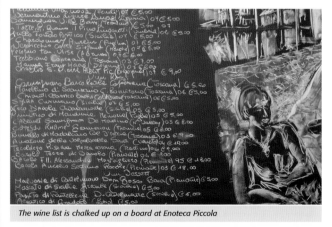

The wine list is chalked up on a board at Enoteca Piccola

popular sister pub around the corner at Via dell'Olmata 43.

➕ K6 ✉ Via San Martino ai Monti 28
☎ 06 4890 4781 🕐 Daily 5pm–2am
🚇 Cavour 🚌 75, 84, 117 to Via Cavour or 16, 70, 71, 360 to Piazza Santa Maria Maggiore

ENOTECA PICCOLA
This intimate wine bar, close to Piazza Navona, is ideal for a romantic interlude.

➕ E5 ✉ Via del Governo Vecchio 74–75
☎ 06 6880 1746 🕐 Daily 11am–2am
🚌 46, 62, 64 to Corso Vittorio Emanuele II

A great spot for an evening drink

ENOTECA TRASTEVERE
This tavern-like wine bar has more than 900 wines. On weekends, a pianist plays jazz and swing. There are tables outside in summer.

➕ F7 ✉ Via della Lungaretta 86 ☎ 06 588 5659 🕐 Mon–Tue, Thu–Sat 6pm–2am, Sun 5pm–1am 🚌 H, 75, 175 to Piazza Sidney Sonnino

ESCOPAZZO
www.escopazzo.it
Intimate, late-night wine and cocktail bar just off Piazza Venezia, with DJ sets, occasional live music and a warm, relaxed atmosphere.

➕ G6 ✉ Via d'Aracoeli 41 ☎ 389 683 5618 🕐 Tue–Sun 10pm–5am 🚌 40, 64, 170 and other services to Piazza Venezia

FRENIE FRIZIONI
www.freniefrizioni.com
A fixture at the heart of Trastevere since 2005, this sleek, modern bar

offers the chance to drink and eat light meals either in the pared-down interior or at tables in the small piazza outside.

➕ E7 ✉ Via del Politeama 4-6 ☎ 06 4549 7499 🕐 Daily 6.30pm– 2am 🚌 H,8 to Viale di Trastevere

NUOVO SACHER
www.sacherfilm.eu
Although dedicated to Italian film talent, this cinema occasionally shows foreign films in *versione originale* on Monday. Seats up to 360 people; in summer there are screenings in the courtyard.

➕ F8 ✉ Largo Ascianghi 1 ☎ 06 581 8116 🕐 Daily 6–9.30 🚌 H, 8 to Viale di Trastevere 💲 Moderate

OPPIO CAFFÈ
www.oppiocaffe.it
Old, vaulted brick walls are offset

MUSIC OUTDOORS

Alfresco recitals often take place throughout the city in summer. Locations include the cloisters of Santa Maria della Pace; the Villa Doria Pamphilj; in the grounds of the Villa Giulia; and the Area Archeologica del Teatro di Marcello from July to September (as part of the Estate al Tempietto, also known as the Concerti del Tempietto, www.tempietto.it). Venues are subject to change.

Enjoy an evening of classical music

RIPARTE CAFÉ

www.riparte.com

This stylish café and lounge is part of the four-star Ripa hotel, located in a quiet spot near the Tiber between Via Portuense and Viale di Trastevere. It makes a great place for an early cocktail or aperitif. There is occasional live music on Friday and Saturdays.

🔳 E9 ⊠ Via degli Orti di Trastevere 1 ☎ 06 58611 🕐 Bar-café 10.30am–11.30pm, restaurant 12.30–2.30, 7.30–11 🚌 H, 8

STADIO OLIMPICO

Home to Rome's two big football teams, AS Roma and Lazio. Games are played here alternate Sundays.

🔳 Off map ⊠ Via del Foro Italico ☎ 06 323 7333 (box office) or 06 36851 🚇 Ottaviano, then bus 32 to Piazzale della Farnesina

AS Roma information:
Tickets available at many outlets around Rome. They are non-transferable; photo ID required to enter the stadium. A full list of sellers is available on the official AS Roma website at www.asromastore.it. Also from Lottomatica stores and AS Roma outlets (⊠ Piazza Colonna 360 ☎ 06 69992 4643)

Lazio information:
Tickets can be bought online at www.sslazio.it. Also at Lottomatica stores or Lazio Style outlets (details at www.sslazio.it) ⊠ Via Farini 34 ☎ 06 482 6768

by contemporary fittings in this airy café-bar-club on the street immediately north of the Colosseum, by the Colle Oppio park. There are wonderful floodlit views of the amphitheatre plus live music some nights, and DJs most Fridays and Saturdays.

🔳 J7 ⊠ Via delle Terme di Tito 72 ☎ 06 474 5262 🕐 Wed–Mon 7am–2am; closed in Aug

PIPER

www.piperclub.it

A very famous club. Open since the 1960s, Piper is consistently popular, thanks partly to its music policy of changing with the times.

🔳 L1 ⊠ Via Tagliamento 9 ☎ 06 855 5398 🕐 Fri–Sat 11pm–5am 🚌 63, 86, 92 to Via Tagliamento 💷 Very expensive

---

APERITIVO TIME

The great Torinese predilection for the pre-dinner *aperitivo* has arrived in Rome. Arrive after 7pm and you can feast or graze on generous snacks of pasta, cold meats, couscous, cheese and much more all for the price of a glass of wine. Popular *aperitivo* bars are opening all the time. One of the longer established is Etabli (⊠ Vicolo delle Vacche 9, ☎ 06 9761 6694; www.etabli.it, Mon—Wed 6.30pm—1am, Thu—Sat 6.30pm—2am).

Laws are more liberal in Italy than in many countries. The legal age for buying alcoholic drink in bars or shops is 18, but it's rare for proof of age to be demanded. Laws against drinking and driving, however, are firmly enforced. Opening times for licensed premises are not set, and correspond to the opening times of each establishment. The only occasion on which restrictions on opening are fixed are before, during and after some football matches.

STRAVINSKY BAR

www.hotelderussie.it

Picasso and the writer Jean Cocteau whiled away hours in these gardens, now the setting for a pretty, if expensive hotel bar.

🕂 G3 ⊠ De Russie Hotel, Via del Babuino 9 ☎ 06 689 1694 🕔 Daily 9am–1am 🚇 Flaminio 🚌 117, 119

TEATRO OLIMPICO

www.teatroolimpico.it

The Filarmonica di Roma performs here, as well as other international dance and music ensembles.

🕂 Off map at F1 ⊠ Piazza Gentile da Fabriano 17 ☎ 06 323 4890; Box Office 06 326 5991 🚌 910 Pannini

TEATRO DELL'OPERA DI ROMA

www.operaroma.it

One of Italy's top opera houses; also an official venue for ballet. Summer performances are staged outdoors in the Terme di Caracalla.

🕂 J–K5 ⊠ Piazza Beniamino Gigli 1 ☎ 06 4816 0255 or 06 481 7003 🚇 Termini 🚌 H, 40, 60, 64, 70, 71, 170 to Via Nazionale or services to Termini

TEATRO VASCELLO

www.teatrovascello.it

On the edge of Trastevere, this is a small but good venue for experimental dance and some classic ballet, and multimedia events.

🕂 D8 ⊠ Via Giacinto Carini 78 ☎ 06 588 8031 🕔 Sep–Jun Tue–Sat 5.30–9, Sun 3–5 🚌 44, 75, 710, 870

TRINITY COLLEGE

www.trinity-rome.com

One of the better historic pubs in the *centro storico*. It serves inexpensive food as well as Guinness.

🕂 G5 ⊠ Via del Collegio Romano ☎ 06 678 6472 🕔 Daily noon–3am 🚌 62, 63, 85, 95, 117, 119 to Via del Corso and all services to Piazza Venezia

LA VINERIA REGGIO

The quainter side of night-time drinking. Old-fashioned inside, with characters to match. Try the popular Drunken Ship pub close by.

🕂 F6 ⊠ Campo de' Fiori 15 ☎ 06 6880 3268 🕔 Mon–Sat 8.30am–2am, Sun 5pm–2am; closed in Aug 🚌 46, 62, 64 to Corso Vittorio Emanuele II or 70, 81, 87 to Corso del Rinascimento

Wine bar in Trastevere

Eat

There are places to eat across the city to suit all tastes and budgets. In this section establishments are listed alphabetically.

Introduction

In Rome, prepare yourself for rich, sun-drenched tastes. Thousands of restaurants cater to every budget and provide every kind of dining experience. Eating is so much a social way of life that it is quite normal to spend several hours over a meal.

What to Eat

Rome is devoted to Italian food, and not the relatively sophisticated food of Bologna or Milan, but a cuisine that has its roots in simple, peasant cooking. Staples from elsewhere in the country are available, not least pizza, but the classic Roman dishes are offal (brains, tripe), salt cod, veal, chickpeas and pigs' trotters. Wines are robust and unpretentious, typically the refreshing and inexpensive whites such as Frascati from the Albani hills south of the city.

Where to Eat

Central Rome's restaurants are concentrated in the streets around Piazza Navona and the Pantheon. Trastevere is also a traditional dining area, along with the more outlying Testaccio and San Lorenzo. Romans now demand value for money, resulting in the return of traditional trattorias and osterias, plus the emergence of informal wine bars *(enoteche)*, salad bars, bars with food and Italian-style diners. The food may often be simple, but culinary standards are higher than they were five or ten years ago.

CUTTING COSTS

In bars, you will pay less for food and drink if you stand at the bar rather than sitting at waiter-service tables. Most have a selection of rolls *(panini)* and sandwiches *(tramezzini)*. For tap, rather than bottled water, ask for 'acqua dal rubinetto, per favore'. Pizza by the slice makes a good lunchtime snack—tiny establishments can be found across the city: look for signs 'Pizza al Taglio' or 'Pizza al Forno'. Many *alimentari* (small food shops) will make up a round Roman roll *(una rosetta)* with cheese or ham.

Pizza or pasta, whatever your choice; visit a deli for delicious bread for a picnic; start the day with a cappuccino

Directory

The Ancient City

Bars by Day
San Clemente
Coffee/Pastries
Antico Caffè del Brasile
Fine Dining
Antonello Colonna
Fish/Seafood
San Teodoro
Roman/Italian
Agata e Romeo
Il Bocconcino
Pasqualino
Silvio alla Suburra

Central Rome

Bars by Day
Caffè della Pace
Salotto 42
Vineria Reggio
Coffee/Pastries
Caffè Farnese
Sant'Eustachio
La Tazza d'Oro
Fine Dining
Al Bric
Il Convivio Troiani
Il Pagliaccio
Fish/Seafood
La Rosetta
Gelaterie
Gelateria della Palma
Tre Scalini
Pizza/Pasta
Da Baffetto

Roman/Italian
Antica Birreria Peroni
Il Bacaro
Da Francesco
Ditirambo
Grano
'Gusto
Maccheroni
Terra di Siena
World Cuisines
L'Eau Vive

Trastevere and the South

Bars by Day
Friends Art Café
Coffee/Pastries
Bibli
Fine Dining
Checchino dal 1887
Glass Hosteria
Gelateria
Alberto Pica
Pizza/Pasta
Da Vittorio
Dar Poeta
Ivo
Panattoni
Roman/Italian
Augusto
Casetta de' Trastevere
Checco er Carettiere
Da Felice
Da Lucia
Giggetto
Paris
Piperno
Sora Lella
Vecchia Roma

Northern Rome

Fine Dining
Le Jardin de Russie
Gelateria
Il Gelato di San Crispino
Roman/Italian
Matricianella
Pizza/Pasta
Est! Est! Est!

Vatican and Around

Fine Dining
La Pergola
Roman/Italian
Borgo Nuovo
Dal Toscano
Taverna Angelica

Further Afield

Roman/Italian
Antico Ristorante Sibilla
Cacciani
Il Grottino della Sibilla dal 1826
Priscilla
Zarazà

Eating A-Z

PRICES

Prices are approximate, based on a 3-course meal for one person.

€€€	over €50
€€	€30–€50
€	under €30

AGATA E ROMEO €€€

www.agataeromeo.it

It is worth putting up with a less-than-perfect position south of Termini because this homey, one Michelin-star, family-run restaurant serves some of the city's best and most imaginative modern Roman cooking. The *tagliata di tonno* (slices of tuna) followed by the delightful *millefoglie* for dessert stand out.

➕ K6 ✉ Via Carlo Alberto 45 ☎ 06 446 6115 🕐 Tue–Fri 12.30–2.30, 7.30–10; Sat, Mon 7.30–11pm, closed 1–27 Jan, 6–28 Aug 🚌 70, 71, 360 to Via Carlo Alberto

ALBERTO PICA €

Alberto Pica offers around 20 varieties of excellent-quality ice cream; try their specialities such as green apple *(mele verde)* and Sicilian citrus *(agrumi di Sicilia)*.

➕ F6 ✉ Via della Seggiola 12 ☎ 06 686 8405 🕐 Mon–Sat 8.30am–2am (also Sun 4pm–2am Apr–Oct); closed 2 weeks in Aug 🚌 8 to Via Arenula and 8, 46, 62, 63, 64, 70, 87, 186, 492 to Largo di Torre Argentina

AL BRIC €€

This stylish *osteria* and wine bar close to Campo de' Fiori offers creative Mediterranean cooking and a choice of 1,000 wines. Desserts are especially appetizing.

➕ E6 ✉ Via del Pellegrino 51–52 ☎ 06 687 9533 🕐 Tue–Sun 7.30–midnight; closed 2 weeks in Aug 🚌 8, 64, 87 and other services to Largo di Torre Argentina

ANTICA BIRRERIA PERONI €

www.anticabirreriaperoni.net

Ideal for a simple lunch or dinner featuring classic Roman cooking. There is a large beer hall.

➕ G5 ✉ Via di San Marcello 19 ☎ 06 679 5310 🕐 Mon–Sat 12–12 🚌 63, 75, 81, 84, 87 and all other buses to Piazza Venezia

ANTICO CAFFÈ DEL BRASILE €

A superb variety of beans and ground coffee is sold from huge sacks or at the bar. Try the 'Pope's blend': John Paul II bought his coffee here before his pontificate.

➕ J6 ✉ Via dei Serpenti 23 ☎ 06 488 2319 🕐 Mon–Sat 6am–8.30pm, Sun 7am–8pm; closed Sat from 2pm and Sun Jun–Aug 🚌 60, 63, 64, 70, 117, 170 to Via Nazionale or 75, 84, 117 to Via Cavour

ANTICO RISTORANTE SIBILLA €€€

www.ristorantesibilla.com

Enjoys a glorious setting by Tivoli's

THE MENU

Starters are called antipasti; first course (soup, pasta or risotto) is *il primo*; and main meat and fish dishes are *il secondo*. Salads *(insalata)* and vegetables *(contorni)* are ordered (and often eaten) separately. Desserts are *dolci*, with cheese *(formaggio)* or fruit *(frutta)* to follow. If no menu card is offered, ask for *la lista* or *il menù*. A set-price menu *(un menù turistico)* may seem good value, but portions are usually small and the food is invariably poor—usually just spaghetti with a tomato sauce, followed by a piece of chicken and fruit.

circular Temple of Vesta, overlooking the Aniene gorge. Dishes might include *cannelloni alle tre carni* (cannelloni with a three-meat filling) and *agnello scottadito con la cicoria* (grilled lamb with chicory).

➕ Off map ✉ Via della Sibilla 50, Tivoli ☎ 0774 335281 ⏲ Daily 12.30–3, 7–10.30; closed Mon in Nov

ANTONELLO COLONNA €€–€€€

www.antonellocolonna.com

Celebrated chef Antonello Colonna has earned repeated Michelin stars for his sophisticated cooking in this futuristic, virtually all-glass restaurant in the Palazzo delle Esposizioni. Go for the good-value 'City Lunch' from Tuesday to Friday (choose from two menus at €15) .

➕ H5 ✉ Via Milano 9a – corner of Via Nazionale ☎ 06 4782 2641 ⏲ Tue–Sat 12–3, 7.20–10.30, Sun 12.20–3.30 🚌 40, 60, 64, 70, 71 and other services to Via Nazionale

AUGUSTO €

One of Trastevere's last remaining inexpensive and authentic family-run trattorias, with simple, classic Roman cooking. No credit cards.

➕ E7 ✉ 10 ✉ Piazza de' Renzi 15 ☎ 06 580 3798 ⏲ Daily 12–3.30, 8–11; closed Aug 🚌 23, 280 to Lungotevere Sanzio or H, 8 to Piazza Sidney Sonnino

IL BACARO €€€

www.ilbacaroroma.com

This tiny but gracious restaurant can be noisy, but the light, modern, pan-Italian cooking is great. You must reserve ahead.

➕ F5 ✉ Via degli Spagnoli 27, near Piazza delle Coppelle ☎ 06 687 2554 ⏲ Daily 12–12; closed Aug 🚇 Spagna 🚌 117, 119

Dining in style

BIBLI €€

www.bibli.it

This Trastevere bookshop-cum-cafeteria is particularly popular for Sunday brunch. A selection of pastas, quiches, couscous and vegetable dishes are served buffet style.

➕ F7 ✉ Via dei Fienaroli 28 ☎ 06 581 4534 ⏲ Tue–Sun 11am–midnight, Mon 5.30–midnight buffet-style dinner 🚌 H, 23, 44, 56, 75, 280 to Viale di Trastevere or Piazza Sidney Sonnino

IL BOCCONCINO €

www.ilbocconcino.com

A recent but traditional-looking trattoria, offering classic Roman dishes, though service may be slow at busy times. It is one of several good options in the grid of streets east of the Colosseum —also try Café Café for snacks and light lunches or Luzzi for pizzas, both just seconds away at Via di San Giovanni in Laterano 44 and 88 respectively.

➕ J7 ✉ Via Ostilia 23 ☎ 06 7707 9175 ⏲ Thu–Tue 12.30–3, 7–11; closed 2 weeks in Aug 🚌 All services to the Colosseum

EAT

Traditional pizzas at Da Baffetto

BORGO NUOVO €€

www.ristoranteborgonuovo.it
Ideal after a visit to St. Peter's or
Vatican Museums for a quiet sit
down and some freshly prepared
Italian food. Meat, fish, pizza and
pasta dishes feature on the menu
alongside salads and sandwiches.
🞢 D4 ✉ Borgo Pio 104 ☎ 06 689 2852
🕐 Daily 12–10; closed Tue Nov–Mar
Ⓜ Ottaviano 🚌 81 to Piazza del
Risorgimento

CACCIANI €€

www.cacciani.it
An established restaurant serving
Roman and classic Italian dishes.
Try the house specialty, *pollo alla
romana* (Roman-style chicken with
a tomato sauce). Also a hotel.
🞢 Off map ✉ Via A. Diaz 13, Frascati
☎ 06 940 1991 🕐 Tue–Sun 12.30–2.30,

7–10.30; closed Sun evening Oct–May, and
7–14 Jan, 16–26 Aug

CAFFÈ DELLA PACE €

www.caffedellapace.it
This is a trendy bar, which is quieter by day, when you can enjoy
light snacks outside or admire the
19th-century mahogany interior.
🞢 F5 ✉ Via della Pace 3–7, off Piazza
Navona ☎ 06 686 1216 🕐 Tue–Sun
8.30am–2am, Mon 4pm–2am (Aug daily
5pm–2am, but closed 13–20 Aug) 🚌 30,
70, 87, 116 to Corso del Rinascimento

CAFFÈ FARNESE €

Quieter and more elegant than the
bars on nearby Campo de' Fiori,
this café serves cakes, ice creams
and light snacks as well as drinks.
There are tables outside on the
cobbled street.
🞢 E6 ✉ Via dei Baullari 106–107, corner
Piazza Farnese ☎ 06 6880 2125 🕐 Daily
7am–2am 🚌 8, 46, 62, 64

CASETTA DE' TRASTEVERE
€–€€

This curious but appealing restaurant at the heart of Trastevere has
tables outside on a quiet square.
There is additional seating in an
interior that recreates a traditional
Roman piazza, complete with
balconied houses. Straightforward
Roman cooking at fair prices.
🞢 E7 ✉ Piazza de' Renzi 31a–32 ☎ 06
580 0158 🕐 Daily 12–3, 7–12 🚌 H, 23,
280 to Ponte Sisto-Piazza Trilussa

UNUSUAL WAITRESSES

You are served at the L'Eau Vive (▷ 146) by nuns from an order known as the Vergini
Laiche Cristiane di Azione Cattolica Missionaria per Mezzo del Lavoro (Christian Virgins of
Catholic Missionary Action through Work). With restaurants in several parts of the world,
their aim is to spread the message of Christianity through the medium of French food. At
9.30pm, during dinner, the nuns sing Ave Maria.

EAT

CHECCHINO DAL 1887 €€€

www.checchino-dal-1887.com

Robust appetites are required for the menu at this Testaccio establishment. Quintessential Roman dishes relying largely on offal are the speciality. There is outdoor seating during the summer. Reservations are advisable.

🔳 Off map G9 ⊠ Via Monte Testaccio 30 ☎ 06 574 6318 🕙 Tue–Sat 12.30–3, 8–11; closed Aug, 24 Dec–2 Jan 🚌 3, 60, 75, 118 to Piramide

CHECCO ER CARETTIERE €€–€€€

www.checcoercarettiere.it

A Trastevere beacon to traditional cooking surveyed by black and white photos of celebrities. Good seafood and home-made specialities feature. Outside patio and internal garden room for smokers.

🔳 E7 ⊠ Via Benedetta, 10–13 ☎ 06 581 7018 🕙 Daily 12.30–3, 7.30–11 🚌 23, 115, 125 or tram 8 to Piazza Trilussa

IL CONVIVIO TROIANI €€€

www.ilconviviotroiani.com

The Troiani brothers from Italy's Le Marche region have created a tranquil little restaurant with a reputation for innovative and subtle-tasting modern dishes.

🔳 F4 ⊠ Vicolo dei Soldati 31 ☎ 06 686 9432 🕙 Mon–Sat dinner only 8–10.30; closed 13–17 Aug 🚌 30, 70, 87, 116, 492 to Corso del Rinascimento

DA BAFFETTO €

www.pizzeriabaffetto.it

A tiny, hole-in-the-wall pizzeria that has retained its atmosphere and low prices. Thin, crisp pizzas fired in a traditional oven are the speciality. Very popular so expect to wait for a table. There is a new outlet near Campo de' Fiori at Piazza del Teatro di Pompeo 18 (tel 06 6821 0807; daily 12.30–3, 6.30–1am).

🔳 E5 ⊠ Via del Governo Vecchio 114 ☎ 06 686 1617 🕙 Daily 6.30pm –1am; closed in Aug 🚌 46, 62, 64 to Corso Vittorio Emanuele II

DA FELICE €€

www.feliceatestaccio.com

This Testaccio institution has been smartened up since the retirement of Felice, and the trattoria fare is as good as ever.

🔳 Off map G9 ⊠ Via Mastro Giorgio 29, Testaccio ☎ 06 574 6800 🕙 Mon–Sat 12.30–3, 8–11.30; closed Sun and 3 weeks in Aug 🚌 Tram to Via Marmorata

DA FRANCESCO €

A simple restaurant near Piazza Navona, which over the years has never lost its appeal, thanks to a warm, friendly atmosphere, good Roman food and low prices. There are no reservations, so it's best to arrive early.

🔳 E5 ⊠ Piazza del Fico 29 ☎ 06 686 4009 🕙 Wed–Mon 12–3, 7–1, Tue 7pm–1am 🚌 64 and other services to Chiesa Nuova on Corso Vittorio Emanuele II

DA LUCIA €

www.trattoriadalucia.com

A traditional trattoria tucked away between Santa Maria in Trastevere and Santa Maria della Scala, with a lively, mixed clientele.

🔠 E7 ⊠ Vicolo del Mattonato 2b
☎ 06 580 3601 ⏰ Tue–Sun 12.30–2.30, 7.30–10.30 🚌 H, 23, 280 to Ponte Sisto-Piazza Trilussa

DA VITTORIO €

A tiny Neapolitan-run Trastevere pizzeria that makes a good standby if Ivo (▷ 148) is busy.

🔠 E7 ⊠ Via di San Cosimato 14a, off Piazza San Calisto ☎ 06 580 0353 ⏰ Daily 11am–11.30pm 🚌 H, 8 to Viale di Trastevere

DAL TOSCANO €–€€

www.ristorantedaltoscano.it

This large trattoria north of Piazza San Pietro serves Tuscan food, and is particularly known for its meats and its wood-fired grill.

🔠 C3 ⊠ Via Germanico 58/60 ☎ 06 3972 5717 ⏰ Tue–Sun 12.45–3, 8–11.15 🚇 Ottaviano 🚌 23, 49, 81 to Piazza del Risorgimento

DAR POETA €

www.darpoeta.com

A popular and long-established pizzeria hidden in a quiet street. The interior is simple but pizza and desserts are creative and excellent.

🔠 E7 ⊠ Vicolo di Bologna 45 ☎ 06 588 0516 ⏰ Daily 12–11 🚌 8, 870 and all services to Trastevere

DITIRAMBO €€

www.ristoranteditirambo.it

The kitchen in this small restaurant near Campo de' Fiori uses organic ingredients, and produces home-made bread, pasta and desserts. Italian cooking with a creative twist. Reservations are essential.

🔠 F6 ⊠ Piazza della Cancelleria 72 ☎ 06 687 1626 ⏰ Tue–Sun 1–3, 7.30–11.30, Mon 8pm–11.30pm; closed part of Aug 🚌 46, 62, 64, 87, 116, 492 to Corso Vittorio Emanuele II

L'EAU VIVE €€

www.ristorante-eauvive.it

Expect a bizarre but heavenly dining experience. Predominantly French food is served by nuns. Politicians, celebrities and locals also enjoy the beautiful 16th-century frescoed dining rooms.

🔠 F5 ⊠ Via Monterone 85 ☎ 06 6880 2101 ⏰ Mon–Sat 12.30–3.30, 7.30–10; closed Aug 🚌 8, 46, 62, 63, 64, 70, 87, 186, 492 to Largo di Torre Argentina

EST! EST! EST! €

www.anticapizzeriaricciroma.com

This is among Rome's oldest and best pizzerias.

🔠 J5 ⊠ Via Genova 32 ☎ 06 488 1107 ⏰ Mon–Fri 12–3, 7–11.30; closed Aug 🚇 Repubblica 🚌 H, 40, 60, 64, 70, 117, 170 to Via Nazionale

FRIENDS ART CAFÉ €

www.cafefriends.it

A lively and welcoming café and bar that is a good bet at any time of the day for *panini*, salads, pastas, meat dishes, snacks and light meals. It's especially popular at *aperitivo* hour.

🔛 E7 ✉ Piazza Trilussa 34 ☎ 06 581 6111 🕙 Mon–Sat 7.30am–2am, Sun 6pm–2am 🚌 H, 23, 280 to Ponte Sisto-Piazza Trilussa

GELATERIA DELLA PALMA €

A big, brash place north of the Pantheon near the Trevi Fountain. Cakes and chocolates, plus more than 100 varieties of ice cream—many of them a little wild.

🔛 F5 ✉ Via della Maddalena 20 ☎ 06 6880 6752 🕙 Daily 8.30am–midnight or later 🚌 116 to Piazza della Rotonda

IL GELATO DI SAN CRISPINO €

www.ilgelatodisancrispino.com

Probably the best ice cream in Rome. A second outlet has opened at Piazza Maddalena 3, just north of the Pantheon.

🔛 H4 ✉ Via della Panetteria 42 ☎ 06 679 3924 🕙 Mon–Thu noon–12.30am, Fri–Sat 11am–1.30am, Sun 12.30–12 🚇 Barberini

GIGGETTO €

www.giggettoalportico.it

A famous Romano-Jewish restaurant in the Ghetto district, in business for over 80 years. Try the classic *carciofi alla giudea* (Jewish-style artichokes).

🔛 G6 ✉ Via Portico d'Ottavia 21a ☎ 06 686 1105 🕙 Tue–Sun 12.30–2.30, 7.30–11;. closed late Jul, Aug 🚌 H, 8, 63 to Via Arenula and 46, 62, 63, 70 and other services to Largo di Torre Argentina

GLASS HOSTERIA €€€

www.glass-restaurant.it

The contemporary styling of this striking restaurant is a world away from that of the traditional Roman trattoria. The adventurous design is matched by excellent, creative Italian cooking that earned a Michelin star in 2011.

🔛 E7 ✉ Vicolo delle Cinque 58 ☎ 06 5833 5903 🕙 Tue–Sun 8pm–11.30pm 🚌 H, 23, 280 to Ponte Sisto-Piazza Trilussa

GRANO €€

www.ristorantegrano.it

You'll either love or hate the virtually all-white decor of this faux-rustic bar and restaurant just east of San Luigi dei Francesi. The menu features excellent pastas and homemade breads, plus innovative, southern Italian, cooking.

🔛 F5 ✉ Piazza Rondanini 53 ☎ 06 6819 2096 🕙 Daily 12.30–3, 7.30–12 🚌 70, 80, 87, 116 and other services to Corso del Risorgimento

IL GROTTINO DELLA SIBILLA DAL 1826 €

Well-priced, simple and tasty regional food presented in two

BUYING ICE CREAM

Ice cream *(gelato)* in a proper *gelateria* (ice-cream shop) is sold either in a cone *(un cono)* or a paper cup *(una coppa)*. Specify which you want and then decide how much you wish to pay: Sizes of cone and cup go up in price bands, usually starting small and ending enormous. You can select up to two or three varieties (more in bigger tubs) and will usually be asked if you want a swirl of cream *(panna)* to round things off.

intimate dining rooms or a terrace in summer. The wine and olive oil used is home-produced.

➕ Off map ✉ Piazza Rivarola 21, Tivoli ☎ 0774 332 606 🕐 Tue–Sun 12.30–2.30, 7–10; closed 15 Dec–8 Jan

'GUSTO €€

www.gusto.it

A chic, modern restaurant on two levels where you can eat pizzas, salads and other light meals downstairs or fuller meals upstairs. There is also a book store and kitchenware shop.

➕ F3 ✉ Piazza Augusto Imperatore 9 ☎ 06 322 6273 🕐 Daily 12–3, 7.30–12 🚌 117, 119 to Via del Corso

IVO €

The best-known of Trastevere's pizzerias. Lines are common but turnover is quick.

➕ E7 ✉ Via di San Francesco a Ripa 158 ☎ 06 581 7082 🕐 Wed–Mon 5.30pm–1am; closed 3 weeks Aug 🚌 H, 8, 780 to Viale di Trastevere

LE JARDIN DE RUSSIE €€€

www.hotelderussie.it/dining

Inspired Mediterranean cuisine. Dine in the garden by candlelight for a memorable experience.

➕ G3 ✉ Via del Babuino 9 ☎ 06 3288 8870 🕐 Daily 12.30–2.30, 7.30–10.30 🚇 Flaminio 🚌 81, 88, 95, 117, 224, 490

MACCHERONI €€

www.risorantemaccheroni.com

A popular and informal restaurant close to the Pantheon, spread through several attractive, rustic dining rooms (plus tables outside on a small square). Attentive staff and good, traditional Italian dishes.

➕ F5 ✉ Piazza delle Coppelle 44 ☎ 06 6830 7895 🕐 Daily 12.30–3, 7–11.30 🚌 8, 64, 87 and other services to Largo di Torre Argentina and Via del Corso

MATRICIANELLA €€

www.matricianella.it

This delightful trattoria has been in business since 1957, conveniently close to Via del Corso, in a side street not far from the parliament building. It offers Roman cooking with the odd twist and has a few outside tables in summer.

➕ G4 ✉ Via del Leone 4 ☎ 06 683 2100

A tempting plate of pasta

Mon–Sat 12.30–2.30, 7.30–11; closed Sun and 3 weeks in Aug 116 to Via della Scrofa and all services to Via del Corso

IL PAGLIACCIO €€€

www.ristoranteilpagliaccio.it

Inventive chef Anthony Genovese was awarded his first Michelin star in 2007 and a second in 2009, and this gourmet experience continues to be a superb combination of Mediterranean, Oriental and traditional Italian cuisine.

E5 Via dei Banchi Vecchi 129 06 6880 9595 Wed–Sat lunch and dinner; Tue dinner; closed Sun, Mon, part Jan, Aug

PANATTONI €

Big, bright and often busy, Panattoni is known locally as 'L'Obitorio' (The Morgue) on account of its characteristic cold marble-topped tables. Watch the flamboyant chef flip the pizzas at the oven. Arrive early to secure a table outside.

F8 Viale di Trastevere 53 06 580 0919 Thu–Tue 7pm–2am; closed 3 weeks in Aug H, 8, 780 to Viale di Trastevere

PARIS €€

www.ristoranteparis.com

A popular and elegant little restaurant known for its fish, pastas and Roman cuisine. Outside tables for alfresco dining. Reserve ahead.

E7 Piazza di San Calisto 7a 06 581 5378 Tue–Sun 12.30–7.30, 8–11, Mon 8–11; closed 3 weeks in Aug H, 8 to Piazza Sidney Sonnino or 23, 280 to Lungotevere Sanzio

PASQUALINO €€

A simple, long-established trattoria with good, robust food a few minutes east of the Colosseum.

K7 Via SS. Quattro Coronati 66 06 700 4576 Tue–Sun 12–3, 7–11; closed 2 weeks in Aug Colosseo 85 to Via di San Giovanni in Laterano

LA PERGOLA €€€

www.romecavalieri.com

Chef Heinz Beck's panoramic restaurant at the Rome Cavalieri is Rome's only three Michelin-starred establishment. The elegant dining room is a splendid setting for the taster menu, which is a spectacular taste of heaven.

Off map A1 Via Cadlolo 101 06 3509 2152 Tue–Sat dinner only 7.30–11; closed 1–28 Jan, 10–25 Aug

PIPERNO €€

www.ristorantepiperno.com

Much Roman cuisine is based on the city's Jewish culinary traditions. The famous and resolutely traditional Piperno has been a temple to Romano-Jewish cuisine for over a century. Reserve ahead.

F6 Via Monte de' Cenci 9 06 6880 6629/ 2772 Tue–Sat 12.45–2.20, 7.45–10.20, Sun 12.15–3; closed Aug H, 8, 63 to Via Arenula and 8, 46, 62, 63, 64, 70, 87, 492 to Largo di Torre Argentina

PRISCILLA €

www.trattoriapriscilla.com

Small, family-run trattoria that offers classic Roman dishes, including *carciofi alla romana* (artichokes) and *pappardelle al sugo di cinghiale* (large pasta ribbons with wild boar sauce).

➕ Off city centre map ✉ Via Appia Antica 68 ☎ 06 513 6379 ⏱ Mon–Sat 12.30–3, 8–12, Sun 12.30–3. Closed part Feb and Aug

LA ROSETTA €€€

www.larosetta.com

An exclusive fish and seafood restaurant whose popularity means reservations are a must.

➕ F5 ✉ Via della Rosetta 8–9 ☎ 06 686 1002 ⏱ Daily 12.45–2.45, 7.30–11; closed 3 weeks in Aug 🚌 119 to Piazza della Rotonda or 70, 87, 90 to Corso del Rinascimento

SALOTTO 42 €

www.salotto42.it

Relaxed place for drinks or light meals during the day; in the evening it's a stylish cocktail bar.

➕ G5 ✉ Piazza di Pietro 42 ☎ 06 678 5804 ⏱ Tue–Sun 10am–2am (earlier Sun); closed part of Aug 🚌 C3, 62, 63, 85, 91

SAN CLEMENTE €

This bar/pizzeria is a great place to refuel between the Colosseum and the basilica of San Giovanni in Laterano. Three vaulted rooms and a terrace offer inexpensive food.

RESTAURANT ETIQUETTE

Italians have a strong sense of how to behave, which applies in restaurants as much as anywhere. It is considered bad form to order only one course in more sophisticated restaurants—if that is what you want, go to a pizzeria or *trattoria*.

➕ K7 ✉ Via di San Giovanni Laterano 124 ☎ 06 7045 0944 ⏱ Mon–Sat 7am–2am, Sun 8am–2am 🚇 Colosseo or San Giovanni 🚌 85, 87, 117 to Via di San Giovanni in Laterano

SAN TEODORO €€€

www.st-teodoro.it

Set among the medieval houses in the shadow of the Forum, this established restaurant specializes in fish and seafood. Dine alfresco on traditional delights and lighter dishes. Reserve ahead.

➕ H7 ✉ Via dei Fienili, 49–51 ☎ 06 678 0933 ⏱ Mon–Sat 1–3, 8–11 🚇 Colosseo

SANT'EUSTACHIO €

www.santeustachioilcaffe.it

Excellent coffee served in a pleasant interior and at tables outside. One of Rome's best.

➕ F5 ✉ Piazza Sant'Eustachio 82 ☎ 06 6880 2048 ⏱ Daily 8.30am–1am 🚌 119 to Piazza della Rotonda or 30, 70, 87, 116 to Corso del Rinascimento

SILVIO ALLA SUBURRA €

www.osteriadellasuburra.com

A simple restaurant in a quiet street a few minutes' walk from the Colosseum. Pastas are homemade and there's a good house wine from the Frascati Hills.

➕ J6 ✉ Via Urbana 67–69 ☎ 06 486531 ⏱ Tue–Sun 12.45–3, 7–11 🚇 Cavour

SORA LELLA €€–€€€

www.soralella.com

Founded by the actress Sora Lella, and now presided over by her son and nephews, this is a former *trattoria* on the Isola Tiberina. Roman cooking, with menu and daily specials. The *gnocchi all' amatriciana* are excellent.

➕ G7 ✉ Via di Ponte Quattro Capi 16

Breakfast in Rome is washed down with a cappuccino or the longer and milkier *caffè latte*. At other times espresso (*un caffè*), a short kick-start of caffeine, is the coffee of choice or *caffè macchiato*, with a drop of milk—Italians never drink cappuccino after lunch or dinner. Decaffeinated coffee is *caffè Hag* and iced coffee *caffè freddo*.

☎ 06 686 1601 🕓 Mon–Fri 12.30–5.30, 7.30–11, Sat–Sun 12.30–11; closed 15–20 Aug 🚌 23, 23, 63, 280 to Lungotevere dei Cenci or Lungotevere degli Anguillara

TAVERNA ANGELICA €€
www.tavernaangelica.it
Delicate, innovative cooking and a minimalist interior.
✚ D4 ✉ Piazza Amerigo Capponi 6 ☎ 06 687 4514 🕓 Mon–Sat 7pm–midnight, Sun 12.30–2.30, 7.30–midnight; closed 2 weeks in Aug Ⓜ Ottaviano 🚌 23 to Via San Porcari

LA TAZZA D'ORO €
www.tazzadorocoffeeshop.com
Probably the city's best espresso and *granita di caffè* (coffee ice).
✚ G5 ✉ Via degli Orfani 84 ☎ 06 678 9792 🕓 Daily 7am–8pm 🚌 119 to Piazza della Rotonda or 30, 70, 87, 116, 186 to Corso del Rinascimento

TERRA DI SIENA €€
www.ristoranteterradisiena.com
Tuscan specialities served close to Piazza Navona, with outside tables in a pretty square in summer.
✚ F5 ✉ Piazza di Pasquino 77–78 ☎ 06 6830 7704 🕓 Mon–Sat 12.30–2.30, 7.30–10.30. Sun lunch and dinner in Dec 🚌 40, 46, 62, 64 and other services to Largo di Torre Argentina

TRE SCALINI €
www.ristorante-3scalini.com
Known for its chocolate-studded *tartufo* (the best chocolate-chip ice cream) served with cream.

✚ F5 ✉ Piazza Navona 28–32 ☎ 06 6880 1996 🕓 Sun–Fri 10am–midnight, Sat 10am–3am 🚌 30, 70, 87, 116 and other services to Corso del Rinascimento

VECCHIA ROMA €€
www.ristorantevecchiaroma.com
Popularity has not spoiled this pretty, predominantly fish restaurant at the heart of the Ghetto, with outdoor dining in summer or in the 18th-century interior.
✚ G6 ✉ Piazza dei Campitelli 18 ☎ 06 686 4604 🕓 Mon–Tue, Thu–Sun 1–3, 8–11; closed 3 weeks in Aug 🚌 44, 46, 60 and other services to Piazza Venezia or Via del Teatro di Marcello

VINERIA REGGIO €
The oldest wine bar on the Campo, splendid for soaking up the atmosphere from tables spilling onto the street. Sandwiches and snacks are complemented by a selection of fine wines.
✚ F5 ✉ Campo de' Fiori 15 ☎ 06 6880 3268 🕓 Mon–Sat 9am–2am, Sun 4pm–2am; closed 2 weeks in Aug 🚌 Many services to Corso Vittorio Emanuele II or Largo di Torre Argentina

ZARAZÀ €
Appealing terrace and three attractive dining rooms, where you can enjoy traditional Roman cooking with a light touch.
✚ Off map ✉ Via Regina Margherita 45, Frascati ☎ 06 942 2053 🕓 Tue–Sun 12.30–2.30, 7.30–10.30; closed Sun 7.30–10.30 Oct–May and 3 weeks in Aug

EAT

SLEEP

Sleep

Rome has accommodation to suit everyone, ranging from luxurious and modern upmarket hotels to simple, budget B&Bs. In this section establishments are listed alphabetically.

SLEEP

Introduction

Following Rome's renaissance in the wake of the Jubilee Year in 2000, the number of luxury five-star hotels in the city is now almost double what it was. Previously crumbling *palazzi* and many of the longer-established hotels have been restored.

Location, Location

As in any city, Rome has a wide range of accommodation types, from small, low-budget places around Termini station to grand, five-star luxury establishments on the Via Vittorio Veneto. What to expect in terms of price and quality depends largely on location. Staying in the *centro storico* means that you are close to all of Rome's sights, but also to its sounds. Narrow streets and tall buildings tend to amplify the noise. Quiet places can be found, on the edge of the popular areas or in hotels with double glazing. If you really value your sleep, book a room in the quieter Aventino, Celio or Prati districts. You will have to travel, but public transport is inexpensive, and hotels are often cheaper than in the heart of the city.

What You Get for Your Money

The familiar star system operates in Italy, with five stars denoting the highest standard of comfort, luxury and facilities. A one-star hotel has few facilities and frequently does not include a private bathroom. Normally both television and telephone will be in the lobby. These establishments tend not to accept credit cards and do not have a 24-hour desk service.

RESERVATIONS

Reserve well in advance, especially if your stay is over the peak periods, which tend to be the greater part of the year. January to March and August are the least crowded months and you should be able to get some deals in this period—consult hotel websites. If you arrive without a reservation, do ask to see the room before you commit.

From the top: The pretty, ivy-covered Raphaël; entrance of the Hotel Trastevere; help with the luggage; a grand entrance welcomes visitors at this hotel

Directory

The Ancient City

Budget
Perugia
Mid-Range
Bolivar
Celio
Nerva
Luxury
Capo d'Africa

Central Rome

Budget
Navona
Pomezia
Smeraldo
Mid-Range
Abruzzi
Albergo Cesari
Campo de' Fiori
Due Torri
La Residenza Farnese
Santa Chiara

Luxury
Raphaël

Trastevere and the South
Budget
Trastevere

Northern Rome
Budget
58 Le Real de Luxe
B&B 3 Coins
Mid-Range
Casa Howard
Locarno
Manfredi
Quirinale
Luxury
Art
De Russie
Hassler-Villa Medici
Regina Hotel Baglioni

Sleeping A-Z

PRICES

Prices are approximate and based on a double room for one night.

€€€	over €300
€€	€150–€300
€	under €150

58 LE REAL DE LUXE €
www.58viacavour.it
A B&B with attention to detail. The 16 rooms are beautifully furnished, combining gleaming bedsteads with crystal chandeliers and leather armchairs with plasma-screen TV and big walk-in showers.

🚇 K5 ✉ Via Cavour 58 ☎ 06 482 3566 or 06 482 1638 🚋 Cavour or Termini

ABRUZZI €€
www.hotelabruzzi.it
There are 25 large rooms, some with a view of the Pantheon; rooms at the rear are quieter.
🚇 F5 ✉ Piazza della Rotonda 69 ☎ 06 679 2021 🚋 119 to Piazza della Rotonda or 46, 62, 63, 64, 70, 87, 186 to Largo di Torre Argentina

ALBERGO CESARI €€
www.albergocesari.it
A friendly and straightforward three-star hotel with a loyal clientele, 47 elegant rooms and a

fabulous roof garden/terrace. There has been a hotel here since 1787. In an excellent position at the heart of the historic city.

➕ G5 ✉ Via di Pietra 89a ☎ 06 674 9701 🚌 60, 62, 85, 117, 119, 160 to Via del Corso

ART €€€

www.hotelartrome.com

A long minimalist white marble corridor provides access to the entrance hall of this latest addition to the glamorous Spanish Steps area. High-tech furnishings and bright hues blend with parquet floors and hand-stiched leather. The luxurious bathrooms feature glass, metal, and mosaic tiles.

➕ G3 ✉ Via Margutta 56 ☎ 06 328 711 🚇 Spagna

B&B 3 COINS €

www.3coinsbb.com

Three coins and three wishes for this modest but welcoming B&B round the corner from the Trevi Fountain. The seven bedrooms vary in size, are pleasantly furnished and have good facilities.

➕ G4 ✉ Via dei Crociferi 26 ☎ 06 446 0434, reservations 06 4977 3153 🚌 Many services to Via del Tritone

BOLIVAR €€

www.bolivarhotel.com

This four-star hotel is perfectly positioned for sights of the Ancient City, in a quiet alley just off busy Via IV Novembre. There are 30 spacious, recently renovated rooms. Breakfast is taken on the roof terrace.

➕ H6 ✉ Via della Cordonata 6, between Via IV Novembre and Via XXIV Maggio ☎ 06 679 1614 🚇 Barberini 🚌 H, 40, 60, 64, 70, 117, 170 to Via IV Novembre or Via Nazionale

CAMPO DE' FIORI €€

www.hotelcampodefiori.com

Good value and position close to Campo de' Fiori. The 27 rooms are rather small and vary in decor, from exposed brick to funky red and green colours. The roof garden is a pleasant bonus.

➕ F6 ✉ Via del Biscione 6 ☎ 06 6880 6865 🚌 46, 62, 64 to Corso Vittorio Emanuele II

Most rooms in the Hotel de Russie overlook the terrace and gardens

CAPO D'AFRICA €€€

www.hotelcapodafrica.com
Close to the Colosseum, this designer boutique hotel boasts sleek contemporary decor, with sunny, bright shades and displays of Italian modern art. Roof terrace.
➕ K7 ✉ Via Capo d'Africa 54 ☎ 06 772 801 🚇 Colosseo

CASA HOWARD €€

www.casahoward.com
Split into two houses, both near the Piazza di Spagna, this boutique hotel offers 10 stylish rooms. The location is excellent for shopping and the sights near the Spanish Steps and Trevi Fountain.
➕ G4 ✉ Via Capo le Case 18 ☎ 06 6992 4555 🚇 Spagna 🚌 116, 117, 119, 590 to Via dei Due Macelli or all services to Via del Tritone

CELIO €€

www.hotelcelio.com
In an enviable spot close to the Colosseum, this stylish and funky hotel has 19 spacious rooms, each distinguished by large frescoes of Renaissance themes. Rooms on the upper floor have Jacuzzis.
➕ J7 ✉ Via dei Santissimi Quattro 35/c ☎ 06 7049 5333 🚇 Colosseo

DE RUSSIE €€€

www.hotelderussie.it
A glorious hotel just off Piazza del Popolo that is distinguished by its modern and stylish design. The 122 rooms are calm and bright, and most have views of the

NOISE

Noise is a fact of life in every Roman hotel, whatever the price category. Surveys have shown Rome to be the noisiest city in Europe. It is difficult to escape the cacophony entirely (unless the hotel is air-conditioned and windows are double-glazed), but to lessen the potential racket you should avoid rooms overlooking main thoroughfares and the area around Termini in favour of rooms looking out on parks or obscure back streets. Also ask for rooms away from the front of the hotel or facing on to a central courtyard *(cortile)*.

delightful gardens, a lovely spot to dine alfresco.
➕ F3 ✉ Via del Babuino 9 ☎ 06 328 881 🚇 Flaminio 🚌 117, 119 to Piazza del Popolo

DUE TORRI €€

www.hotelduetorriroma.com
A real find, in a perfect position hidden in a tiny alley between Piazza Navona and the Tiber. The 26 adequate rooms vary from stylish to plain. Some have small terraces with good views.
➕ F5 ✉ Vicolo del Leonetto 23–25 ☎ 06 6880 6956 🚌 30, 70, 81, 87, 116, 186 to Lungotevere Marzio or Corso del Rinascimento

HASSLER-VILLA MEDICI €€€

www.hotelhasslerroma.com
You'll find this well-located, long-time jet-set and VIP haunt just above the Spanish Steps. There are 95 rooms and 8 suites.

SLEEP

AGENCIES

A good source of all kinds of accommodation, from hotels to bed-and-breakfasts in all price ranges, is Enjoy Rome (tel 06 445 1843 or 06 445 6890; www.enjoyrome.com). The company also offers walking and specialist tours.

⊞ H4 ✉ Piazza Trinità dei Monti 6 ☎ 06 699 340 Ⓜ Spagna 🚌 119 to Piazza di Spagna

LOCARNO €€

www.hotellocarno.com

In a quietish side street close to Piazza del Popolo, this hotel has genuine 1920s art nouveau decor, with a feel of old-world elegance, along with nice touches such as an open fire in winter and a garden and delightful roof terrace. Ask for the better rooms in the eastern annexe, not the downbeat rooms in the main building.

⊞ F3 ✉ Via della Penna 22 ☎ 06 361 0841 Ⓜ Flaminio 🚌 926 to Via di Ripetta, or 81 to Lungotevere in Augusta

MANFREDI €€

www.hotelmanfredi.it

A quiet, family-run hotel with charming service and 18 pretty rooms, in a cobbled street of galleries and antiques shops.

⊞ G3 ✉ Via Margutta 61 ☎ 06 320 7676 Ⓜ Spagna 🚌 119 to Piazza di Spagna

NAVONA €

www.hotelnavona.com

Twenty-six simple rooms, friendly owners and a superb central loca-tion, in a 15th-century palazzo.

⊞ F5 ✉ Via dei Sediari 8 ☎ 06 6830 1252 🚌 30, 70, 87, 116, 186 to Corso del Rinascimento

NERVA €€

www.hotelnerva.com

In an unbeatable position for the sights of the Ancient City—the Nerva is one of only a few hotels that are within a stone's throw of the Roman Forum. Renovated rooms, some with original features, amiable service and a warm welcome awaits.

⊞ H6 ✉ Via Tor de'Conti 3–4 ☎ 06 678 1835 Ⓜ Colosseo or Cavour 🚌 60, 84, 85, 87, 175 and all other services to Via dei Fori Imperiali, Piazza Venezia or Via IV Novembre-Via Nazionale

POMEZIA €

www.hotelpomezia.it

Close to Piazza Navona, with 17 small rooms (some have private bathrooms), with a roof terrace and small bar. There is a specially adapted room for people with disabilities, but no lift.

⊞ F6 ✉ Via dei Chiavari 12 ☎ 06 686 1371 🚌 46, 62, 64 to Corso Vittorio Emanuele II or 8, 46, 62, 63, 64, 70, 80 to Largo di Torre Argentina

QUIRINALE €€

www.hotelquirinale.it

Composers such as Puccini and Verdi have stayed at the charming four-star Quirinale. High-ceiling rooms are sensitively refurbished in the neoclassical style, with chan-deliers, parquet floors, early empire

WHAT TO PAY

Hotels are classified by the Italian state into five categories from one star (basic) to five stars (luxury). The prices each can charge are set by law and must be displayed in the room (you will usually find them on the door). However, prices within a hotel can vary from room to room (and some hotels have off- and peak-season rates). If a room is too expen-sive, do not be afraid to ask for a less expensive one. Watch for extras like air-conditioning and obligatory breakfasts. Single rooms cost about two-thirds the price of doubles, and to have an extra bed in a room adds 35 per cent to the bill.

furnishings and huge bathrooms. Breakfast taken in the shaded loggia overlooking the courtyard is a delight.

➕ J4 ✉ Via Nazionale 7 ☎ 06 4707 🚇 Repubblica

RAPHAËL €€€

www.raphaelhotel.com

An intimate, charming and ivy-covered hotel, hidden away yet near Piazza Navona. The 55 rooms are elegantly furnished with classic taste. Reserve ahead.

➕ F5 ✉ Largo Febo 2 ☎ 06 682 831 🚌 70, 81, 87 to Corso del Rinascimento

REGINA HOTEL BAGLIONI €€€

www.baglionihotels.com

Murano glass chandeliers, silk tapestries and marble bathrooms are just some of the luxury fixtures and fittings in this lovely Liberty-style hotel. The Sala Belvedere on the eighth floor has glass walls and a large sun roof with splendid views. Service and attention to detail are exemplary.

➕ H3 ✉ Via Vittorio Veneto 72 ☎ 06 421 111 🚇 Barberini

LA RESIDENZA FARNESE €€

www.residenzafarneseroma.it

The hotel is in a superb position in an ivy-hung alley and in the shadow of the great Palazzo Farnese. Part of a former convent, the rooms vary from modest former nuns' cells with small bathrooms to large, pastel-decorated salons.

➕ E6 ✉ Via del Mascherone 59 ☎ 06 6821 0980 🚌 116 to Via Giulia and Via dei Farnesi

SANTA CHIARA €€

www.albergosantachiara.com

Run by the same family since 1830; some rooms can be dark but the location, in a side street immediately south of the Pantheon, is superb.

➕ F5 ✉ Via Santa Chiara 21 ☎ 06 867 2979 🚌 8, 46, 62, 63, 64, 70, 80 to Largo di Torre Argentina

SMERALDO €

www.smeraldoroma.com

Thirty-five plain and clean rooms, in a back street close to Campo de' Fiori.

➕ F6 ✉ Vicolo dei Chiodaroli 11 ☎ 06 687 5929 🚌 46, 62, 64 to Corso Vittorio Emanuele II or 8, 46, 62, 63, 64, 70, 80 to Largo di Torre Argentina

TRASTEVERE €

www.hoteltrastevere.net

This hotel has 20 bright rooms, all with private bathrooms, plus four apartments.

➕ E7 ✉ Via Luciano Manara 24a–25 ☎ 06 581 4713 🚌 H, 8 to Piazza Sonnino or Viale di Trastevere

SLEEP

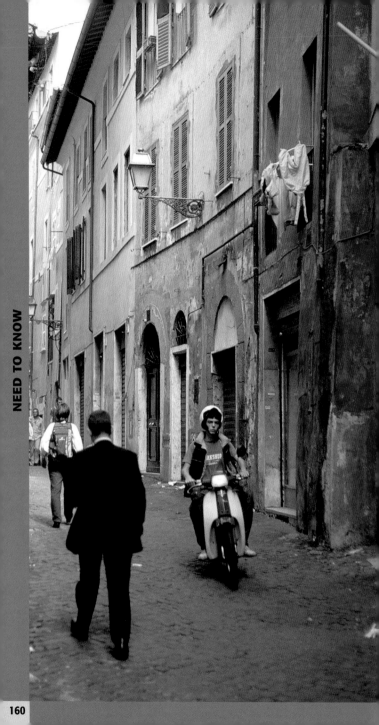

Need to Know

This section takes you through all the practical aspects of your trip to make it run more smoothly and to give you confidence before you go and while you are there.

NEED TO KNOW

Planning Ahead

WHEN TO GO

The best time to visit Rome is April to early June or mid-September to October, when the weather is not uncomfortably hot. Easter weekend is very busy. Many restaurants and businesses close for the entire month of August. January and February are the quietest months.

TIME

Italy is one hour ahead of GMT in winter, six hours ahead of New York and nine hours ahead of Los Angeles.

TEMPERATURE

JAN	FEB	MAR	APR	MAY	JUN	JUL	AUG	SEP	OCT	NOV	DEC
44°F	46°F	52°F	58°F	64°F	74°F	79°F	77°F	72°F	64°F	55°F	48°F
7°C	8°C	11°C	14°C	18°C	23°C	26°C	25°C	22°C	18°C	13°C	9°C

Spring (March to April) can be muggy. It can be rainy in April and May.

Summer (June to August) is hot and dry, with sudden thunderstorms. July and August are uncomfortably hot.

Autumn (September to November) is mixed but can produce crisp days with clear skies.

Winter (December to February) is short and moderately cold.

WHAT'S ON

January *La Befana* (6 Jan): Epiphany celebrations; fair and market in Piazza Navona.

February *Carnevale* (week before Lent): Costume festivities; parties on Shrove Tuesday.

March *Festa di San Giuseppe* (19 Mar): Street stalls in the Trionfale area north of the Vatican.

April *Good Friday* (Mar/Apr): Procession of the Cross at 9pm to the Colosseum, led by the Pope. *Easter Sunday:* The Pope addresses the assembled crowds at noon in Piazza di San Pietro.

May *International Horse Show* (early May): Concorso Ippico in Villa Borghese.

June *Festa della Repubblica* (2 Jun): Military parade along Via dei Fori Imperiali.

July *Tevere Expo* (last week Jun/Jul): Food and handicrafts fair on the banks of the Tiber.

August *Ferragosto* (15 Aug): Feast of the Assumption; everything closes for at least the day.

September *Art Fair*: Via Margutta. *Sagra dell'Uva* (early Sep): Wine and harvest festival in

the Basilica di Massenzio.

October *Antiques Fair* (mid-Oct): Via dei Coronari.

November *Ognissanti* (1–2 Nov): All Saints' Day. *Festa di Santa Cecilia* (22 Nov): In the catacombs and church of Santa Cecilia in Trastevere.

December *Festa della Madonna Immacolata* (8 Dec): Pope and other dignitaries leave flowers at the statue of the Madonna in Piazza di Spagna. *Christmas Eve Midnight Mass*: The most striking are at Santa Maria Maggiore and Santa Maria in Aracoeli.

ROME ONLINE
www.060608.it
Rome's official website for tourist information has mostly generalized information on the city.

www.adr.it
The official site of Rome's main airports, Fiumicino and Ciampino, with useful contacts and details of transport links to the city.

www.vatican.va
Vatican City's polished official website offers multilingual information on the Vatican Museums, the Sistine Chapel and St. Peter's, a calendar of religious events, an online version of its official newspaper and other general information on the Vatican.

www.comune.roma.it
Aimed primarily at tourists, the official website of Rome's city council contains transport and other useful general information.

www.romaclick.com
A general site useful for checking up-to-the-minute information on events and exhibitions. It offers a user-friendly accommodation reservation service with last-minute reductions.

www.romeguide.it
An Italian-based site with a wealth of daily updated information; use it for reserving museum passes and to find out what's on.

www.enjoyrome.com
This friendly English-language site is run from Rome and has a quirkier approach than most; use it for general information, as well as tips on discovering Rome on foot and by public transport. Excellent links and daily updates.

www.museionline.it
An informative and easy-to-navigate site that will fill you in on what the city's museums have to offer. Lots of practical information as well. Opening times and prices are not always current.

GOOD TRAVEL SITES
www.atac.roma.it
Rome's bus company website gives every scrap of information about public transport, including maps and how to buy the best ticket for your needs—Italian and English.

www.capitolium.org
Devoted to the Roman and Imperial forums, this site includes a wide range of historical material, including reconstructions of how the forums might have looked in their original state.

www.catacombe.roma.it
The official site of Rome's catacombs.

www.fodors.com
A travel-planning site where you can research prices and weather, book tickets, cars and rooms, and ask questions; links to other sites.

INTERNET CAFÉS
Much of central Rome is covered by a free, city-funded wireless network. New users need to register and enter—and have—a mobile phone number. For further information tel 06 6919 0720; www.romawireless.com.

Globalservice
✉ F7 ✉ Piazza Sidney Sonnino 27
☎ 06 5833 3316
🕐 Daily 9am–10pm

Getting There

VISAS AND INSURANCE

Check visa and passport requirements before travelling, see www.gov.uk or italy.usembassy.gov.

EU citizens with an EHIC card are entitled to the same cover for medical treatment as Italian residents (for which they may still have to pay); insurance to cover illness and theft is still strongly advised. Visitors from outside the EU should check their insurance coverage and, if necessary, buy a supplementary policy.

TIPS

● Avoid taxi and hotel touts who will approach you at the airport. Use only licensed (white) taxis.
● Buy your return (round-trip) train ticket when you arrive at Fiumicino. The lines are much longer at Termini, and the ticket will not become valid until you stamp it on your return journey.
● You will find suitcases with wheels a godsend at Fiumicino. It is quite some distance between baggage reclaim and the exit, and for some stretches you cannot use a baggage trolley, particularly on the homeward journey.

AIRPORTS

There are direct flights into Rome from Europe and North America to Leonardo da Vinci and Ciampino airports. Visitors from Europe can also arrive by rail to Stazione Termini, or by bus to Stazione Tiburtina.

32km (20 miles) • **24km (15 miles)** • **16km (10 miles)** • **8km (5 miles)** • **Rome**

Leonardo da Vinci Airport
36km (22 miles) to city centre
Train 31 min, €14

Ciampino Airport
15km (9 miles) to city centre
Bus/Metro 35 min

FROM LEONARDO DA VINCI AIRPORT

Scheduled flights arrive at this airport 36km (22 miles) southwest of the city, better known as Fiumicino (tel switchboard 06 65951). The website for both main Rome airports is www.adr.it. The most efficient way to reach the heart of Rome from the airport is by rail into Stazione Termini. Trains leave every 30 or 60 minutes (6.36am–11.36pm) at 6 and 36 minutes past the hour and take about 30 minutes. Catch the Leonardo Express service direct to Termini, not the service via Fara Sabina. Buses (www.sitabusshuttle.it) depart from Terminal 3 outside train hours and take up to 50 minutes to Rome's Termini and Tiburtina train stations. Taxis take from 30 minutes to two hours depending on traffic, and are expensive (€48 set fare, maximum four passengers, including luggage, to points within the Aurelian Walls). Take only licensed cabs (white) or a prepaid car with driver available from Terminal 1 (tel 800 017 387) or Terminal 3 (tel 06 6501 1122).

FROM CIAMPINO

This smaller airport, which handles mostly low-cost and charter flights, is 15km (9 miles) southeast of the city. There are good facilities but the airport does not have a direct rail link to the heart of Rome. To get there take a 15-minute bus journey by COTRAL bus to the Metro (underground) station at Anagnina, then the 20-minute journey to Termini on Metro line A. Taxis take 30 to 40 minutes and cost around €45. Bus shuttles (tel 06 9761 0632; www.terravision.eu) serve various no-frills and other airlines' flights and run to Termini (€4 one-way, €8 round-trip booked online, otherwise €6/ €11).

ARRIVING BY BUS

Most long-distance buses terminate at Tiburtina, to the northeast of the city. Although the station is some way out of the city, it is well served by the Metro (line B) to Termini or Colosseo and by numerous bus services (for example. No. 492 to the centre). Eurolines run buses from more than 100 European cities. For details of routes and tickets, see their website (www.eurolines.com).

ARRIVING BY CAR

In the days of the empire, all roads led to Rome, but in these modern times, all roads lead to the Gran Raccordo Anulare, known as the GRA. This 70km (43-mile) road encircles the city, and is always busy. From Fiumicino airport, take the Autostrada Roma Fiumicino, which leads to the GRA. If you are coming from Ciampino you will need to follow the Via Appia Nuova. From Florence or Pisa, take the A1, also known as the Autostrada del Sole. Visitors arriving from Naples should also use the A1, while those coming from Abruzzo or the Adriatic coast should follow the A24. Wherever you join the GRA, make sure you know which exit you need; your hotel can tell you which one is best.

ARRIVING BY RAIL

Most trains arrive and depart from Stazione Termini, convenient for most of central Rome. Taxis and buses leave from the station fore-court, Piazza dei Cinquecento. For train information tel 892 021; www.trenitalia.com.

DRIVING PERMIT

If you are arriving by car and staying in central Rome, you will need a permit to drive in the city. If you are staying in a hotel, the staff can arrange this for you.

LONG-TERM PARKING

If you are arriving by car, but don't want to use your car in Rome, you can leave it in the long-term parking area (Lunga Sosta) at Fiumicino airport and take the train into the city. Long stay costs €18 (from €5.50 if booked online) for 24 hours or €69 for seven days. Short-stay in 'Multipiano E' costs €30 (from €19 online) daily (tel 06 8898 1981) or €5 hourly.

CAR RENTAL

All major rental firms, and some local ones, have desks at both airports and also in town. Car rental is expensive in Italy and you can often get a better deal if you arrange it before you leave home. The minimum age for renting a car is between 21 and 25 (depending on which company you deal with), and you will need to have held a driver's licence for at least a year. Most firms require a credit card as a deposit. Accident rates are high in Rome, so make sure you have adequate insurance cover. Most car rental contracts include breakdown cover.

Getting Around

VISITORS WITH DISABILITIES

Rome is not an easy place for visitors with physical disabilities. However, the Vatican City has ramps and elevators and some hotels have rooms for visitors with disabilities. Staff at airports, museums and places of interest are willing to help and taxis usually accept wheelchairs, although it is a good idea to phone ahead. The Metro line B is generally accessible (apart from Circo Massimo, Colosseo and Cavour) but the Metro line A and most buses are not. For details contact RADAR (✉ Unit 12, City Forum, 250 City Road, London ECU 8AF ☎ 020 7250 3222; www.radar-shop. org.uk) in the UK or Society for the Advancement of Travel and Hospitality (SATH) (✉ 347 5th Avenue, Suite 610 NY 10016 ☎ 212/447 7284; www.sath.org) in the US.

BUSES

Service is frequent and inexpensive on Rome's mostly green or red-grey regional and blue suburban buses run by ATAC/COTRAL (map ref K4, Piazza dei Cinquecento, tel 06 57003; www.atac.roma.it and www.cotralspa. it; Mon–Sat 8–8; Metro Termini).

The buses are often crowded and slow. Buy BIT tickets (*Biglietto Integrato a Tempo*; €1.50) before boarding, from tobacconists, shops and automatic machines displaying an ATAC sticker. Your ticket must be stamped at the rear of the bus or tram, and is valid for any number of bus rides and one Metro ride within the next 75 minutes. BIG Day (€6), three-day BTI (€16.50) and weekly CIS (€24) passes are available. These need only be validated the first time they are used. Services run 5.30am–11.30pm, depending on the route. The night service consists of buses on key routes midnight–5.30am; night buses have a conductor selling tickets. Remember to enter buses by back doors and to leave by middle doors (if you have a pass or validated ticket with unexpired time you can also use the front doors). Buy several tickets at once as some outlets close early. There are large fines if you are caught without a ticket. Bus stops (*fermate*) list routes and bus numbers, and note that one-way streets often force buses to return along different routes. Note that bus number 64 is especially notorious for pickpockets and that work to extend Rome's Metro means some bus services may follow temporary diversions.

USEFUL SERVICES

● 23 Piazza del Risorgimento (for the Vatican Museums)–Trastevere–Piramide.
● 75 Termini–Roman Forum–Colosseum– Piramide.
● 40, 64 Termini–Piazza Venezia–close to Piazza San Pietro/St. Peter's.
● 110 Open (www.trambusopen.com) Sightseeing service from Stazione Termini to the Colosseum and other key monuments.
● 81 Piazza del Risorgimento (Vatican

Museums)–Piazza Venezia–Circo Massimo.

● 117 Circular minibus service in the historic centre including Piazza Augusto Imperatore–Piazza della Rotonda (Pantheon)–Via del Corso– Piazza di Spagna.

SUBWAY

Rome's subway, the Metro, has two lines, A and B, which intersect at Stazione Termini. Mainly a commuter service and of limited use in the city, it is good for trans-city rides. Station entrances are marked by a large M and each displays a map of the network. Services run 5.30am to 11.30pm (12.30am Saturday). Tickets are valid for one ride (or get a BIT, see 'Buses') and can be bought from tobacconists, bars and shops displaying ATAC or COTROL stickers, and from machines at stations—have euro coins handy.

TAXIS

Official taxis are white, with an official number and a 'Taxi' sign on the roof. Use only these and refuse touts at Fiumicino, Termini and elsewhere. Drivers are not supposed to stop on the streets so it is difficult to hail a cab. Taxis congregate at stands, indicated by blue signs printed with 'Taxi'. Make sure the taxi meter is reset when you start your journey (note one part of the meter will display the minimum fare starting rate). Taxi ranks are available in the area at Termini, Piazza Sidney Sonnino, Pantheon, Piazza di Spagna and Piazza San Silvestro.

Calling a taxi: The company will give you a taxi code name, a number and the time it will take to get to you. The meter starts running as soon as they are called. Companies include: Samarcanda, tel 06 5551, www.samarcanda.it; and centralized Chiamataxi (06 0609). The minimum fare is valid for 3km (2.5 miles) or the first 9 minutes of a ride. Surcharges are levied between 10pm and 7am, all day Sunday, on national holidays, for airport trips (€48 set fare to or from Fiumicino, €30 to or from Ciampino) and for each piece of luggage larger than 35 x 25 x 50cm (13 x 9 x 19in).

HANDY HINT

An integrated ticket, the *Biglietto Integrato Giornaliero* (BIG, €6) is valid for a day's unlimited travel on ATAC buses, the Metro, COTRAL buses and suburban trains (except to Fiumicino airport). *The Carta Integrata Settimanale* pass, or CIS, (€24) is valid for a week as for BIG tickets (see above).

LOST PROPERTY

Report lost or stolen property to a police station, which will issue a signed declaration for your insurance company. The central police station is the Questura
✉ Via San Vitale 15
☎ 06 46861
ATAC lost property
✉ Via Niccolò Bettoni 1
☎ 06 57003
🕐 Mon–Sat 8.30–1
Metro lost property
Line A ☎ 06 487 4309;
Line B ☎ 06 5735 2264
🕐 Mon, Wed, Fri 9–12
COTRAL lost property
Inquire at the route's origin or telephone ☎ 06 57531 or 06 591 5551
Rail lost property
✉ Stazione Termini, Via Giovanni Giolitti 24
☎ 06 4730 6682, daily 7am–10pm
🕐 Mon–Fri 7am–10pm
Airport lost property
☎ Airside 06 6595 3313, otherwise 06 6595 5253

Essential Facts

MONEY

The euro is the official currency of Italy. Banknotes come in denominations of 5, 10, 20, 50, 100, 200 and 500 euros and coins in 1, 2, 5, 10, 20, 50 cents and 1 and 2 euros.

TOURIST INFORMATION

● Azienda di Promozione Turistica di Roma ✉ Via Parigi 11 ☎ 06 488 991/06 060608 🕐 Mon–Sat 8am–7.30pm
● Information kiosks (daily 9–6) are at ✉ Piazza delle Cinque Lune ☎ 06 6880 9240; ✉ Palazzo delle Esposizioni, Via Nazionale ☎ 06 4782 4525; ✉ Lungotevere Castel Sant'Angelo-Piazza Pia ☎ 06 6880 9707

ELECTRICITY
● Current is 220 volts AC, 50 cycles; plugs are the two-round-pin type.

NATIONAL HOLIDAYS
● 1 Jan (New Year's Day)
● 6 Jan (Epiphany)
● Easter Monday
● 25 Apr (Liberation Day)
● 1 May (Labour Day)
● 29 Jun (St. Peter and St. Paul's Day)
● 15 Aug (Assumption)
● 1 Nov (All Saints' Day)
● 8 Dec (Immaculate Conception
● 25 Dec (Christmas Day)
● 26 Dec (St. Stephen's Day)

NEWSPAPERS AND MAGAZINES
● Many Romans read the Rome-based *Il Messaggero*, and the mainstream and authoritative *Corriere della Sera* or the middle-left and populist *La Repubblica* (which has a special Rome edition). Sports papers (such as *Corriere dello Sport*) and weekly news magazines (such as *Panorama* and *L'Espresso*) are also popular.
● Foreign newspapers can usually be bought after 2.30pm on the day of issue from booths *(edicole)* on and close to Termini, Piazza Colonna, Largo di Torre Argentina, Piazza Navona, Via Vittoria Veneto and close to several tourist sights. European editions of major newspapers are also available.

OPENING HOURS
● Shops: Tue–Sat 8–1, 4–8, Mon 4–8 (with seasonal variations) or, increasingly Mon/Tue–Sat 9.30–7.30. Food shops open on Monday morning but may close on Thursday afternoon. Some bookshops open on Sundays.
● Restaurants: daily 12.30–3, 7.30–10.30. Many close on Sunday evening and half- or all day Monday. Most bars and restaurants also have a statutory closing day *(riposo settimanale)* and many close for much of August.
● Churches: variable, but usually daily 7–12,

4.30–7. Most churches close on Sunday afternoon.

● Museums and galleries: vary considerably; usually close on Monday.

● Banks: Mon–Fri 8.30–1.30. Major branches may also open 3–4 and Saturday morning.

● Post offices: Mon–Fri 8.15 or 9–2; Sat 8.15 or 9–12 or 2.

POSTAL SERVICE

● Buy stamps from post offices and tobacconists.

● Post boxes are red and have two slots, one for Rome (marked *Per La Città*) and one for other destinations (*Per Tutte Le Altre Destinazioni*). Newer boxes, usually blue, are for the priority mail service, or *Posta Prioritaria*.

● Vatican post can be posted only in the Vatican's blue *Poste Vaticane* post boxes. The Vatican postal service is quicker (although tariffs are the same), but stamps can be bought only at the post offices in the Vatican Museums. Open as for Vatican Museums (▷ 27) and in Piazza San Pietro, tel 06 6988 3406, Mon–Sat 8.30–6.30

● Main post office (*Ufficio Postale Centrale*) Piazza San Silvestro 19; tel 06 6973 7205, www.poste.it; Mon–Fri 8–7 (Aug Mon–Fri 8–2), Sat 8–1.15

TELEPHONES

● Telephone numbers listed in this book include the city area code (06), which must be dialled even when calling within Rome.

● Public telephones are indicated by a red or yellow sign showing a telephone dial and receiver. They are found on the street, in bars and restaurants and in special offices (*Centri Telefoni*) equipped with banks of phones.

● Phones usually accept phone cards (*schede telefoniche*) available from tobacconists, post offices and some bars in a variety of denominations. Break off the card's corner before use.

● To call Italy from the UK, dial 00 44 and from the US or Canada dial 011, followed by 39 (the country code for Italy) then the number, including the relevant city code.

MEDICAL TREATMENT

There are emergency rooms at these centres: Ospedale Fatebenefratelli ✉ Isola Tiberina ☎ 06 68371; www.fatebenefratelli-isolatiberina.it ✉ Viale del Policlinico 155 ☎ 06 446 2341 or 06 49971; www.policlinicoumberto1.it. The George Eastman Clinic (✉ Viale Regina Elena 287/b ☎ 06 844 831) provides an emergency dentist service. No credit cards.

Pharmacies are indicated by a large green cross. Opening times are usually Mon–Sat 8.30–1, 4–8, but a rotating schedule (displayed on pharmacy doors) ensures at least one is always open. The most central English-speaking pharmacist is Internazionale (✉ Piazza Barberini 49 ☎ 06 487 1195; www.farmint.it).

EMERGENCY NUMBERS

Police, Fire and Ambulance (general SOS) ☎ 112
Police (Carabinieri) ☎ 112
Central Police ☎ 06 46861
UK Embassy ☎ 06 4220 0001
US Embassy ☎ 06 46 471
Telephone Information ☎ 1254 (24 hours), 1254.virgilio.it
International information ☎ 1254 (8am–10.30pm)
ACI Auto Assistance (car breakdowns) ☎ 803 116 (www.aci.it)
General info-tourist line ☎ 06 060608

Words and Phrases

All Italian words are pronounced as written, with each vowel and consonant sounded. Only the letter *h* is silent, but it modifies the sound of other letters. The letter *c* is hard, as in English 'cat', except when followed by *i* or *e*, when it becomes the soft *ch* of 'cello'. Similarly, *g* is soft (as in the English 'giant') when followed by *i* or *e*—*giardino*, *gelati*; otherwise hard (as in 'gas')—*gatto*. Words ending in *o* are almost always masculine in gender (plural: -*i*); those ending in *a* are generally feminine (plural: -*e*). Use the polite second person *(lei)* to speak to strangers and the informal second person *(tu)* to friends or children.

BASICS	
yes	*sì*
no	*no*
maybe	*forse*
OK/alright	*va bene*
please	*per favore*
thank you	*grazie*
many thanks	*mille grazie*
you're welcome	*prego*
excuse me!	*scusi*
when	*quando*
now	*adesso*
why	*perchè*
who	*chi*
may I/can I	*posso*
good morning	*buon giorno*
good afternoon	*buona sera*
good evening	*buona notte*
hello/good-bye (informal)	*ciao*
hello (on the telephone)	*pronto*
I'm sorry	*mi dispiace*
left/right	*sinistra/destra*
open/closed	*aperto/chiuso*
good/bad	*buono/cattivo*
big/small	*grande/piccolo*
with/without	*con/senza*
more/less	*più/meno*
hot/cold	*caldo/freddo*
do you have?	*avete?*
exit	*uscita*
nothing	*niente*
slow	*piano*
fast	*presto/rapido*

NUMBERS	
1	*uno, una*
2	*due*
3	*tre*
4	*quattro*
5	*cinque*
6	*sei*
7	*sette*
8	*otto*
9	*nove*
10	*dieci*
20	*venti*
30	*trenta*
40	*quaranta*
50	*cinquanta*
100	*cento*
1,000	*mille*

COLOURS	
black	*nero*
brown	*marrone*
pink	*rosa*
red	*rosso*
orange	*arancione*
yellow	*giallo*
green	*verde*
light blue	*celeste*
sky blue	*azzuro*
purple	*viola*
white	*bianco*
grey	*grigio*

EMERGENCIES

help!	*aiuto!*
stop, thief!	*al ladro!*
can you help me, please?	*può aiutarmi, per favore?*
call the police/ an ambulance	*chiami la polizia/ un'ambulanza*
I have lost my wallet/passport	*ho perso il mio portafoglio/ il mio passaporto*
where is the police station?	*dov'è il commissariato?*
where is the hospital?	*dov'è l'ospedale?*
I don't feel well	*non mi sento bene*
first aid	*pronto soccorso*

USEFUL PHRASES

how are you? (informal)	*come sta/stai?*
I'm fine	*sto bene*
I do not understand	*non ho capito*
how much is it?	*quant'è?*
do you have a room?	*avete camere libere?*
how much per night?	*quanto costa una notte?*
with bath/shower	*con vasca/doccia*
when is breakfast served?	*a che ora è servita la colazione?*
where is the train/bus station?	*dov'è la stazione ferroviaria/degli autobus?*
excuse me (on bus, train etc)	*mi scusi*
do I have to get off here?	*devo scendere qui?*
where can I buy...?	*dove posso comprare...?*
I would like	*vorrei*
too expensive	*troppo caro*
a table for... please	*un tavolo per... per favore*
excuse me (to attract attention)	*senta*
the bill, please	*il conto, per favore*
we didn't have this	*non abbiamo avuto questo*
where are the toilets?	*dove sono i bagni?*

DAYS/MONTHS

Monday	*lunedì*
Tuesday	*martedì*
Wednesday	*mercoledì*
Thursday	*giovedì*
Friday	*venerdì*
Saturday	*sabato*
Sunday	*domenica*
January	*gennaio*
February	*febbraio*
March	*marzo*
April	*aprile*
May	*maggio*
June	*giugno*
July	*luglio*
August	*agosto*
September	*settembre*
October	*ottobre*
November	*novembre*
December	*dicembre*

TIME AND PLACE

morning	*mattina*
afternoon	*pomeriggio*
evening	*sera*
night	*notte*
today	*oggi*
tomorrow	*domani*
yesterday	*ieri*
early	*presto*
late	*tardi*
later	*più tardi*
when	*quando*
where	*dove*
Where is...?	*Dov'è...?*
Where are we?	*Dove siamo?*
here	*qui/qua*
there	*lì/là*
near	*vicino*
far	*lontano*
on the right	*a destra*
on the left	*a sinistra*

Index

The Automobile Association would like to thank the following photographers and companies for their assistance in the preparation of this book.

2i–3i AA/A Mockford & N Bonetti; **3ii** AA/C Sawyer; **3iii** AA/A Mockford & N Bonetti; **3iv** AA/S McBride; **4–5** AA/A Mockford & N Bonetti; **6t** The Art Archive/Galleria Borghese Rome/ Collection Dagli Orti; **6ct** AA/A Mockford & N Bonetti; **6cb** AA/D Miterdiri; **6/7b–7t** AA/A Mockford & N Bonetti; **7ct** Appollo & Daphne, 1622-25 (Marble), Bernini, Giovanni Lorenzo (1598-1680/Galleria Borghese, Rome, Italy/Giraudon/The Bridgeman Art Library; **7cb–8ct** AA/S McBride; **8cb** AA/A Mockford & N Bonetti; **8/9b** AA/C Sawyer; **9t** AA/P Wilson; **9ct–9cb** AA/C Sawyer; **10l** Getty Images; **10r** AA; **11l** AA/S McBride; **11r** epa european pressphoto agency b.v. / Alamy; **12** AA/A Mockford & N Bonetti; **14/15** AA/S McBride; **15–16/17** AA/A Mockford & N Bonetti; **17tr** AA/S McBride; **17cr** AA/A Mockford & N Bonetti; **18tl** AA/C Sawyer; **18cl–18/19** AA/A Mockford & N Bonetti; **20l** AA/J Holmes; **20/21–23cr** AA/A Mockford & N Bonetti; **24tl** AA/S McBride; **24cl–24/25** AA/J Holmes; **25tr–25cr** AA/C Sawyer; **26tl–26/27c** AA/A Mockford & N Bonetti; **26tr** AA/S McBride; **26cr** AA/P Wilson; **28** AA/A Mockford & N Bonetti; **28/29** AA; **29tr** Massimo Pizzotti/Alamy; **29cr** AA/A Mockford & N Bonetti; **30–30/31** AA/J Holmes; **31** Youth with a Basket of Fruit, 1594 (oil on canvas), Caravaggio Michelangelo Merisi da (1571-1610)/Galleria Borghese, Rome, Italy/Alinari/ The Bridgeman Art Library; **32** AA/C Sawyer; **32/33** AA/A Mockford & N Bonetti; **34** Erin Babnik/Alamy; **34/35–35cra** AA/A Mockford & N Bonetti; **36** AA/P Wilson; **36/37t** AA/J Holmes; **36/37c** AA/P Wilson; **37tr** Judith and Holofernes, 1599 (oil on canvas), Caravaggio, Michelangelo Merisi da (1571-1610)/Palazzo Barberini, Rome, Italy/The Bridgeman Art Library; **37cr** AA/A Mockford & N Bonetti; **38tl** AA/P Wilson; **38cl–38/39** AA/J Holmes; **39** Salome with the head of St. John the Baptist (oil on canvas), Solario, Antonio da (fl.1502-14)/Galleria Doria Pamphilj, Rome, Italy/Alinari/The Bridgeman Art Library; **40–43tr** AA/A Mockford & N Bonetti; **43cr** AA/S McBride; **44** AA/C Sawyer; **44/45ct** AA/A Kouprianoff; **44/45c–45tr** AA/C Sawyer; **45cr** AA/J Holmes; **46** AA/A Mockford & N Bonetti; **46/47ct** AA/S McBride; **46/47c** AA/A Mockford & N Bonetti; **47tr** AA/C Sawyer; **47cr** AA/A Mockford & N Bonetti; **48** AA/A Kouprianoff; **48/49** AA/S McBride; **50** AA/A Mockford & N Bonetti; **50/51ct** AA/J Holmes; **50/51c–51tr** AA/A Mockford & N Bonetti; **51cr** AA/J Holmes; **52–53** AA/A Mockford & N Bonetti; **54** AA/D Miterdiri; **54/55–55tr** AA/C Sawyer; **55cr** image1/Alamy; **56** AA/J Holmes; **56/57** Adam Eastland Rome/Alamy; **57tr** Vito Arcomano/Alamy; **57cr** AA; **58tl** AA/A Mockford & N Bonetti; **58cl** AA/S McBride; **58/59** AA/A Mockford & N Bonetti; **59** AA/A Kouprianoff; **60** AA/D Miterdiri; **60/61ct** AA/A Kouprianoff; **60/61c–61** AA/J Holmes; **62/63** Adam Eastland Italy/Alamy; **63tr** The Art Archive/Museo di Villa Giulia Rome/Gianni Dagli Orti 1; **63cr–64** AA/A Mockford & N Bonetti; **66** AA/T Souter; **67bl** AA/C Sawyer; **67br–71bl** AA/A Mockford & N Bonetti; **71br** AA/A Kouprianoff; **72bl** AA/J Holmes; **72br** AA/A Mockford & N Bonetti; **73bl** AA/J Holmes; **73br–74bl** AA/A Mockford & N Bonetti; **74br** AA/J Holmes; **75–76bl** AA/A Mockford & N Bonetti; **76br** MARKA/Alamy; **77bl** AA/C Sawyer; **77br–78br** AA/S McBride; **79** AA/A Mockford & N Bonetti; **80** AA/A Kouprianoff; **82t** AA/A Mockford & N Bonetti; **82b** AA/D Miterdiri; **83t–86ii** AA/A Mockford & N Bonetti; **86iii** AA/C Sawyer; **86iv** AA/A Mockford & N Bonetti; **86v** AA/A Kouprianoff; **86vi** AA/D Miterdiri; **88t** AA/J Holmes; **88b** AA/A Mockford & N Bonetti; **89t** AA/D Miterdiri; **89b** AA/A Mockford & N Bonetti; **92i** AA/J Holmes; **92ii** AA/D Miterdiri; **92iii** AA/A Mockford & N Bonetti; **92iv** AA/A Kouprianoff; **92v–92vi** AA/C Sawyer; **94t** AA/A Mockford & N Bonetti; **94b** AA/A Kouprianoff; **95t–95b** AA/A Mockford & N Bonetti; **98t** AA/A Kouprianoff; **98b** AA/D Miterdiri; **100–104i** AA/A Mockford & N Bonetti; **104ii–104iii** AA/P Wilson; **104iv–104v** AA/A Mockford & N Bonetti; **104vi** AA/J Holmes; **104vii–106t** AA/A Mockford & N Bonetti; **106b** AA/C Sawyer; **107t–111** AA/A Mockford & N Bonetti; **112t** AA/J Holmes; **112b** AA/P Wilson; **113t–113b** AA/A Mockford & N Bonetti; **116** AA/C Sawyer; **117–120/121t** AA/A Mockford & N Bonetti; **120/121ct** AA/D Miterdiri; **120/121cb–121cbl** AA/C Sawyer; **120/121b** AA/A Mockford & N Bonetti; **123** AA/C Sawyer; **128–130/131ct** AA/A Mockford & N Bonetti; **131ctl** AA/S McBride; **130/131cb** AA/A Mockford & N Bonetti; **131cb** Digitalvision; **130/131b** AA/J Tims; **133** Brand X Pics; **134** AA/A Mockford & N Bonetti; **135** AA/J Holmes; **136** Digitalvision; **137** AA/A Mockford & N Bonetti; **138** AA/C Sawyer; **140i** AA/A Mockford & N Bonetti; **140ii** AA/P Wilson; **140iii** AA/C Sawyer; **140iv** AA/T Harris; **143** AA/A Mockford & N Bonetti; **144** AA/C Sawyer; **148** AA/E Meacher; **152** AA/A Mockford & N Bonetti; **154i–154ii** AA/C Sawyer; **154iii–156** AA/A Mockford & N Bonetti; **160** AA/P Wilson.

Every effort has been made to trace the copyright holders, and we apologise in advance for any unintentional omissions or errors. We would be pleased to apply any corrections in a following edition of this publication.

Rome 25 Best

WRITTEN AND UPDATED BY Tim Jepson
SERIES EDITOR Clare Ashton
COVER DESIGN Chie Ushio, Yuko Inagaki
DESIGN WORK Tracey Butler
IMAGE RETOUCHING AND REPRO Ian Little

Published in the United Kingdom by AA Publishing

ISBN 978-0-8041-4334-9

TENTH EDITION

SPECIAL SALES
This book is available for special discounts for bulk purchases for sales promotions or premiums. For more information, email specialmarkets@randomhouse.com.

Color separation by AA Digital Department
Printed and bound by Leo Paper Products, China

10 9 8 7 6 5 4 3 2 1

A05132
Maps in this title produced from mapping © MAIRDUMONT / Falk Verlag 2013
Further Afield map openstreetmap.org © OpenStreetMap contributors
Transport maps © Communicarta Ltd, UK

Titles in the Series